THE INSIDE SUICIDE:

Copyright© 2012 by Rosemary,
All rights reserved

Library and Archives Canada Cataloguing in Publication

Golding, Rosemary L., 1943-
The inside suicide / Rosemary L. Golding.

Includes bibliographical references and index.
ISBN 978-0-9813593-8-0

1. Golding, Rosemary L., 1943-. 2. Feminism--Religious aspects--Christianity. 3. Women--Canada--Social conditions. 4. Feminists--Canada--Biography. I. Title.

HQ1455.G64A3 2012   305.42092   C2012-905763-0

This edition published by Cybercom Publishing
PO Box 130, Dorset, Ontario Canada P0A 1E0
E-mail: ben@benharrison.ca

Cover, layout and text design: Tim Harrison
Printed and bound in the United States of America and London, England.

Without limiting the rights under copyright reserved above, no part of this publication may be reproduced, stored in or introduced into a retrieval system, or transmitted, in any form or by any means (electronic, mechanical, photocopying, recording or otherwise), without the prior written permission of both the copyright owner and the publisher of this book.

The scanning, uploading, and distribution of this book via the Internet or via any other means without the permission of the publisher is illegal and punishable by law. Your support of the author's rights is appreciated.

Care has been taken to trace the ownership of any copyright material in this text. The publisher will gladly accept any information that will enable them to correct any errors or omissions in subsequent editions.

DEDICATION

This book is dedicated to women who struggle to attain self-knowledge, independence, and freedom from oppression.

Many thanks to my friends and relatives who have encouraged my writing of this work: Mary, Mary, Deanna, Catherine, Betty, Barbara, Lesley, Len, Bill and Jonathan and especially Sheila, for the depth of her understanding and encouragement of my journey toward self-knowledge.

ACKNOWLEGEMENTS

Writing The **Inside Suicide** has been a much longer and more exhausting undertaking than I had ever imagined. It is thanks to many people who have taken the interest, time and effort to help me that this work was written at all.

I would especially like to thank the Harrison-Pennington family for the editing, art work and professional advice in bringing this book to completion. Sheila, thank you for your editing and overall guidance, Timothy, thank you for applying your artistic genius and creativity to the layout and cover design and Ben in overseeing and publishing the entire project.

THE INSIDE SUICIDE: SHATTERING ILLUSIONS

The autumn was gold and crisp; the breeze suspended; the lake shone at the foot of the hill protecting the circling loons, readying for their long flight. My friend described a perfect day at her cottage. She, her husband, with their visiting son and his family, basked in the beauty and peace of the afternoon as they walked the nearby trail, the two young granddaughters, eleven and eight, galloping ahead, whooping down the hill. Suddenly the son called to his eldest daughter: "Sally, slow down! Walk like a young lady!" He turned to his father, exasperated: "I will break her spirit! I will"!

My friend's story chilled me to the bone. I was in a period of intense self-examination of my family background, religion, and my culture; of looking at what made me who I am. Soul-searching in depth. I also had parents, whom I loved and adored at the time, try to break my spirit. Parents who wanted a decorous daughter, an obedient daughter, a good Christian girl! I distinctly remember the sentiment actually being voiced in my childhood home that children had to have their spirits broken. Children were to be seen and not heard. My family was loving, caring, closely knit. Where had the harsh idea that children must be subdued originated?

My friend, aware of my spiritual search, recounted the preceding story for me. She herself has traveled her own road to self-discovery. Her story hit me like an actual physical punch. Her granddaughter has grown up to be a rebel, bless her heart. It has taken me much longer.

Sherry Ruth Anderson and Patricia Hopkins, in their wonderful book, *The Feminine Face of God*, discuss at length the effects of childhood upbringing on one's outlook on life. They quote one woman they interviewed as saying, "When we look into our childhood we often find destiny there. The child has a vision and our parents or society try to stamp it out; so the child has to go underground." (p. 27). I certainly am one who went underground, in my efforts to comply with my parents' expectations.

It has taken years to realize that I am essentially a feminist, have been so subconsciously most of my life, and to understand what being a feminist means to me. It has taken me even longer to realize why I developed as I did along a track which I view now as a form of feminism.

REALIZING MY FEMINISM

I wonder where I was during the '60's when women were 'coming out' on the cusp of the feminist movement, expressing long-held anger at the traditional roles which they and their mothers and sisters had always accepted as proper for themselves. How did I miss the impact of it, considering my bent for individual thinking? I remember that during the latter part of this decade, I was totally engrossed in setting up my career as a high school English teacher, one of the few careers presented to me as an option when I finished my undergraduate university degree in English and Philosophy. There were very few women in those days who considered going into business; even fewer who actually did. Most women needed a more secure path. The idea of doing something as daring as working for a business, and especially of going into business for myself, so untraditional for a woman, was terrifying to me. I didn't even consider it as an option. Brothers, men, did business things. *My* brother went into business. Meanwhile, I could get a good position as a teacher with a public salary, a well-paid 'job' in those days, which I could keep until I got married, when, as my Dad explained, I would always have a career on which to rely if my husband died or became ill. The assumption for me, and for thousands of others like me, was that we would not work after we married, but stay at home supported by our husbands. Discussion of my feelings for the roles into which I was expected to fit my life seems trite to me now, considering the wealth of literature and media attention given to expressing the equality of women today. Nevertheless, even today at this more liberalized stage of my life, feelings of inadequacy arise in me if I do not react as I was taught as a child, that men deserve respect for their attitudes and opinions, simply because they are men. I catch myself back in the meek, submissive role of a woman. Awareness of my childhood programming, and breaking from it, is extremely difficult! The traditions of my family values are still with me, and have stayed with me for most of my career. Other women seem to be able to withstand the onslaughts of living and working in an essentially male world. Why have I had such trouble adjusting? I sense the rebellion in me. I have always valued the importance of individual thinking to such a great extent. Nevertheless, I had a full career teaching, continuing in my field most of my married life, even well past my official retirement. I usually felt satisfied that I was fulfilling my ambitions. I realize now that had I been aware enough, and daring enough to embrace the feminist movement, I would likely have had an even more fulfilling career.

I did not read the feminist writers in those early days. I did not make time to do so, for one thing. My attention was focused almost totally on being good at my job, on conveying scholarship to my students: preparing lessons, marking essays and tests for long hours at night and on weekends. I took delight in helping students understand the literary and emotional intricacies of works like *Macbeth* and *Wuthering Heights*. I knew there was a feminist movement going on. I heard the news, read the papers. I did not relate to this movement of my sisters. My career in itself afforded me a wonderful independence. Why rail against patriarchal systems when I as a woman could get a job that lent me a wonderful independence of which I had only dreamed before? I told myself, 'If you marry, marry a man who understands your need for a career in order for you to feel fulfilled.' And such a man I did marry, but not till I had enjoyed life as an independent woman. What were those feminists complaining about? Besides, at the time, I did not want to be associated with women whom I perceived as angry and troubled, who railed at society's conventions, demonstrated openly, and wrote contentious articles. I would automatically be considered by my coworkers and superiors as angry and outspoken, which would almost certainly have harmed my career. In addition, as a sensitive person, I felt I could not take the dissension and conflict, the criticism which comes from standing out from the crowd by speaking out. To a good extent, I tried to repress my own anger, and usually succeeded. I had long ago as a child learned that compliance, sweetness and agreement with authority were the way to get along well as a woman. I was doing well enough, and enough it seemed to be. But unfortunately I had learned to be afraid of my own power! I still am afraid of it! It terrifies me!

Yet often throughout my career, especially in those early years, I felt depressed, dissatisfied with the seeming shallowness of my life, the lack of substance, even though I was very busy teaching a subject I loved to students whom I enjoyed. Occasionally I would erupt in anger at something in the system, usually at a control of my individuality of teaching style, at lack of appreciation for my hard work. Symptoms of my **Inside Suicide.**

THE INSIDE SUICIDE: SHATTERING ILLUSIONS

I taught in four boards in Ontario. The ones in which I was most unhappy working were the ones which took away my autonomy the most. I needed a sense of pride in my work through my own creative efforts. Occasionally, to my surprise, I was called a 'feminist', which I denied hotly. I valued traditional views of women, even while I subconsciously rebelled against such thinking. I did not want to be associated with 'rabble rousers'. Now, however, I realize that I have always been a latent feminist, subconsciously endorsing feminist views of women and men as equal, having roles which are interchangeable and equally respected.

A PATRIARCHAL UPBRINGING

Where did my concepts of a woman's role in society originally come from? It has taken me a while to realize the depth of the impact of my childhood and parental background. But the ideas I formed of myself as a child were extremely deep, in fact the very marrow of my bones. The concepts we form of ourselves as people are formed in us by our parents and society when we are children.

My dad was a minister in The United Church of Canada. My upbringing was in 'the church'; I was molded in the concept of needing to be a good Christian daughter: going without fail to church and Sunday school weekly, joining church youth groups, going to church camps, listening to my parents' ideas of how I should act in life, the proper, respectable course to take. The course of a *woman*. And I realize now that this kind of training is a subtle form of 'breaking one's daughter's spirit' by putting down her spontaneity and individuality. Boys were allowed so much more action and expression of opinion than we were at that time, in the mid-twentieth century. After much memory-probing over the last few years I have come to the conclusion that in my family, different attitudes towards raising boys and girls stemmed mainly from the church teachings and expectations of my culture, which although strong in my religious home, pervaded the whole fabric of the society in which I was raised. I certainly felt guilt and shame if I failed in pleasing authority. I still do, but am aware of what is happening now. Whose authority? That of my parents and that of the church behind them. And into my adult life, that of my bosses: principals, parents of my students.

Consequently, over the past few years, as I have been delving into the effect of church systems and doctrines, I have gradually realized that the Christian church is based on a system which has skewed women and men in very different directions. To accept the profound impact of this has been very difficult. The church's traditional system, patriarchal, dominated by male attitudes, by expectations of roles of men and women in society, has influenced western civilization's concept of itself in such manifold and subtle ways that we are usually totally unaware of its pervasiveness. The language in all Christian references is still totally masculine, reference to the male God, the Christ, the Church Fathers. Most of the saints are masculine. Most of us accepted completely the church's attitudes to the roles of men and women, attitudes which often have led us into very divergent places in society. Helping enforce this concept of women as subservient caregivers, was the pervasive idea that adherence to the Christian Church is the one and only way to live life well. I accepted with no question my role in society. I tried to fit in, to be meek, deferring to men; even though I felt that their decisions were often faulty, lacking in common sense. I usually succeeded in being a meek and obedient daughter/woman. But sometimes I did not. If I questioned, for example, the fact that one of my school boards was chronically short of books, even though it was well-funded by the government, I was considered a rabble rouser. I felt terribly guilty when I was censured, not understanding why I was criticized for asking questions about organizational problems. I wanted the best for my students. I turned my justifiable anger into guilt.

The people and institutions I tried to please were conceived by, and usually run by men so I considered them right; they were the authority. Therefore I always thought *I must be the one at fault if I didn't fit in.* I had no complete sense of certainty that my own opinions and decisions could be right for me. It was my place in life to agree with what men and administrators decided, to prop up their points of view. I did that automatically. Administrators were usually men. No wonder I sometimes felt anger with my career, even though I knew I was good at my job. My meekness wasn't complete. I still even today occasionally catch myself automatically deferring to men, or to anyone, man or woman, who is in authority. Carolyn G. Heilbrun in *Writing a Woman's Life* has portrayed the problem succinctly: "And, above all other prohibitions, what has been forbidden to women is anger, together with the open admission of desire for power and control over one's life (which inevitably means accepting some degree of power and control over other lives.)" Repressing oneself is an **Inside Suicide!**

THE INSIDE SUICIDE: SHATTERING ILLUSIONS

IMPACT OF DOING WHAT I 'SHOULD' DO

What of my relationship with the church in those early adult years? I went to church only when I was home visiting my family. I tried a few times to go to church in the communities in which I lived, knowing that churches were where communities were forged and bonded, feeling it still my duty to adhere to deeply instilled beliefs and customs of my childhood. I was uncomfortable, however, feeling out-of-place, a stranger. My stomach heaved when I tried. The automatic welcome I had always received as the minister's daughter was no longer there to temper the experience. I went to church because I felt I should; it was the right thing to do. I tried to go because my parents had programmed the expectation in me. But I gradually found that I was feeling dreadfully tired after being at church, and usually slept for hours, unable to concentrate on anything else but the feelings I had experienced there. I would catch myself while in church, sitting in a completely wooden fashion, like a board, unable to move. I made only expected and automatic movements: opening the hymn book, standing to sing, incredibly self-conscious and tense. I tried to obliterate myself as much as possible from other people's consciousness of my presence. I hid within myself. I remember now that these feelings started back in my teenage years, and probably much earlier. I knew I was uncomfortable and stiff, but had no idea why. I could feel the minister's eyes boring right through me, seeing into my soul. I felt everyone else in the congregation watching me, judging me. Telling myself this was ridiculous did not work. I found the atmosphere in a church service, or in any church gathering to be oppressive. I couldn't breathe. I felt utter relief once the service was over and I was released. Yet I still felt delinquent, sinful for not getting out of the church experiences what everyone else seemed to. I felt unable to dedicate myself fully enough to the religious tenets and causes. So I absented myself, and put these feelings out of my mind for years, as much as I could. But I knew that one day I would reexamine the church doctrines that were at the base of my difficulties in accepting the Truth and Wonder of Christian Spiritual Experiences.

THINKING FOR MYSELF

As a result, when I retired from my career, I started reading more on topics I had long boxed in closets: philosophy of religion books from my university courses, and books on the background of church tenets and attitudes. I added new books, many recommended to me by friends and trusted acquaintances: books on feminist teachings, and feminist reactions to Christianity. These were my first independent explorations with real feminism, and I loved them! I felt free, as though I had finally come home! These thought-provoking writers were the only ones I had found so far who were able to explain to me my discomfort with church experiences, my discomfort with myself in society. Many of these writers had searched for their spirituality outside the church. Over the last few years I have tried searching for meaning within the Christian church, which gave me so much of my background. But my comfort level is not there; my need for spirituality is rooted elsewhere. *I realize that I am no longer a Christian in the traditional sense.* I remember when I first realized that I am no longer 'Christian': a real physical shock, an utter fear that I would have no place to which to 'belong'. The sinful feeling of it. Yet, the freedom!

On this rather intensive journey, I have gradually realized that the patriarchal system on which the Christian church is based is one of the main reasons for my disquietude. I always considered patriarchy in my society as proper, as the due of *men*. Patriarchal systems were automatic in my thoughts. Besides, why would a woman want to challenge these traditions? The problems and criticism and ostracism weren't worth it! I knew that if women used their attractiveness and compassion, often they had influential behind-the-scenes roles in society, from which they could wield much power. They did not have to take the front-line risks that men have taken. Why would women want to step into aggressive and combative roles when they could live well in a protected existence, as long as they pleased their husbands? And by extension, as long as they pleased church ideals of family roles in society? But I know now, as I reflect back on my feelings over the years, that I have always felt dishonest trying to fulfill the role of a woman in this way.

AWARENESS

My 'waking' into awareness has been a difficult and long, gradual passage. Yet I did have insights along the way that it is not just women who have been controlled by the church, but men too. They also are thrust by societal conventions into roles created by religions which are still carried on today. Furthermore, I realized that some men are uncomfortable with their expected roles.

Many women wake suddenly, all at once, from a specific incident in their lives, such as the one Sue Monk Kidd describes in detail at the beginning of her wonderful book, *The Dance of the Dissident Daughter*. Whatever the spur to awareness, or the speed of the experience, the incredible difficulty of the journey is always there, for the journey to feminine awareness is a life-changing experience. All that one has known, trusted, believed in as principles in life, is turned up-side-down. Kidd says, "I've given birth to two children, but bringing them into the world was a breeze compared to birthing myself as a woman. Bringing forth a true, intellectual, powerful woman who is rooted in her own feminine center, who honors the sacredness of the feminine, and who speaks the feminine language of her soul is never easy. Neither is it always welcomed. I discovered that few people will rush over to tie a big pink bow on your mailbox." (Kidd, p. 12) I also have found the same emotional reactions in my friends and associates, in my family, in church-going people. I am often looked at in horror. Why would I want to immerse myself in *that* mess? And others try to remind me of the simple beauty of the Christian message. Few understand, or are tolerant of my journey. Fewer still encourage me in it. Fear of what they sense in themselves? Fear that their own 'Sleeping Beauties' may wake up? Fear that if I change, they will in some way have to reexamine their own worlds? And truly it is the fear of rejection which has held me back, and still keeps me silent at times. Fear of hurting others! Such an incredibly strong, limiting emotion, which the church has used to control us to such a huge degree! When I finally realized the extent to which my religion had betrayed me, the pain I felt was extreme! And my anger matched it! I was overcoming my **Inside Suicide.**

DEPENDENCE

How harmful not to be able to be yourself! Maria Callas, for example, was criticized for not continuing her operatic career fully, for not giving it the time it required once she became Aristotle Onassis' mistress. Both Onassis and her singing each required all the passion of her being. She must have been so torn! To sing with the passion she gave her work required her total being. To devote herself to Onassis as she wanted to, was to limit her ability to perform operatic roles. Callas was caught in her acceptance of the view of what a mistress/wife should be.

Look for a minute at Jacqueline Kennedy's life. She attained her place in society *because she was the wife* of John F. Kennedy. Her own style and graciousness helped her image; but she would not have had her goddess status without her marriage. After her husband died, she left the States, fearing for her life, and for those of her children. But a lovely apartment and social connections in Paris were not enough for her to live well. She needed a husband to secure her status. *So* she married Aristotle Onassis, attracted by his fame, social connections, and money. To live with freedom and respect, she required a husband! As a single woman, her life was too limited, and vulnerable. A man in her position would have had unlimited options. How the roles of women have been defined and circumscribed! A woman can live more freely if she has a husband! But what a price, for usually she has to subjugate her own thoughts and opinions, her own *being,* to his. How women have been tied; literally *tied!* both by convention, and by their acceptance of it. How many women have married because of the lure of being cared for?

The most precious thing I have as a person is my independence!

THE SUPPRESSING ROLE OF THE CHURCH

How did our defining roles of a woman develop? It is obvious to me that religious institutions have played a huge role in the social definitions and training of women. While I refer particularly to the Christian church because that is where my training and basic research have been, I feel that other religions have been just as damaging of gender relationships. As I read back into the histories of the early years of Christianity, I realized that clergymen protected their flocks to such an extent that very little individual thinking was allowed. I know now that the church's teachings denied my fundamental right of freedom to search for my own identity, to have individual thought in many areas. The existence of God as *He* is conceived in Jewish and Christian tradition was a topic we discussed, certainly in my home, and in my educational career, and at great length, but most of us did not essentially deny the traditional view of *God* with any seriousness. When I took philosophy at university we all thought of ourselves as broad-minded in discussing controversial Christian doctrine with openness and sometimes vehemence. But I did not allow myself to actually stray from the basic Christian tenets; those who did faced family and community censure. More importantly if I broke from tradition, I would have to face myself as a person, to defend my sense of spirituality for my own personal understanding. Censure from others was too much for me to endure. Forming a spirituality for myself was something I never even considered. So I kept my often differing ideas hidden, suppressed them within, suffered the inner anguish which is often subconscious, and eventually makes people sick. Indeed, I have had to become quite physically ill to realize the depth of my inner anguish, the reasons for my body breaking down.

For most of my life, I had lived in what Sue Monk Kidd calls a Deep Sleep:

> A woman in Deep Sleep is one who goes about in an unconscious state. She seems unaware, or unfazed, by the fact of her female life, the truth about women in general, the way women and the feminine have been wounded, devalued, and limited within culture, churches, and families. She cannot see the wound or feel the pain. She has never acknowledged, or much less confronted,

sexism within the church, biblical interpretations, or Christian doctrine. Okay, so women have been largely missing from positions of church power, we've been silenced and relegated to positions of subordination by biblical interpretations and doctrine, and God has been presented to us as exclusively male. So what? The woman in Deep Sleep is oblivious to the psychological and spiritual impact this has had on her. Or maybe she has some awareness of it all, but keeps it sequestered nicely in her head, rarely allowing it to move down into her heart or into the politics of her spirituality. (Kidd, p. 18).

THE RESULTS OF CONDITIONING

For over two thousand years, many people like me, conditioned by church hierarchy, have embraced churches without realizing how our own power as women has been usurped. By preaching doctrine to people, the traditional church has been able to perpetuate its lack of belief in other people's intellectual abilities. We, as women in particular, have not been allowed to think for ourselves, to form our own opinions. Furthermore, attitudes formed by church teachers have pervaded society's structural beliefs. It is less than 100 years, for example, since women finally gained the right to vote; men considered that our opinions could not be trusted on matters of social importance. Men were the ones who made decisions of importance in the home, and in society. Where did men get this notion of their superior intellectual ability? Patriarchy as taught by religious institutions has changed the roles of men into distorted roles of superiority. As a result they have become the dominant sex in most segments of our modern, 'freethinking' society. Religious teachings enforce this.

The right of women to vote was a right hard won by early twentieth century feminists, those courageous and strong suffragettes who fought and suffered for our right to freedom of expression. The Church, by relegating women to a secondary role, has influenced society's concepts of women's roles to such an invasive extent! My opinion of my own power was devalued, as has been that of so many many other women, my mothers, my grandmothers, and their grandmothers, who passed their ideas down through the generations to me. I hold the Church's influence over society responsible for this to a very large extent. It has made me furious!

Sue Monk Kidd quotes Jungian analyst Sylvia Perera in *Descent to the Goddess: A Way of Initiation for Women* on this topic:

> "What has been valued in the West in women has too often been defined only in relation to the masculine: the good, the nurturing mother and wife; the sweet, docile agreeable daughter; the gently supportive or bright achieving partner. This collective model is inadequate for life; we mutilate, depotentiate, silence and enrage ourselves trying to compress our souls into it

just as surely as our grandmothers deformed their fully breathing bodies into corsets for the sake of an ideal". (Kidd, p. 45)

I have had to remake myself: an agonizing and ongoing process, which does not end or become easier as time goes on. I am still filled with pain and terror, at times excruciating! I fear criticism; I live with fear of rejection. Making myself self-reliant, learning to depend on *myself*, not on an exterior force such as a religion or a god is a never-ending task. I have found this the only way to understand and improve my spiritual, emotional and physical health.

EFFECT OF MASCULINE LANGUAGE

I alluded earlier to the masculine language used in church societies. This accords with the fact that the heroes of spiritual literature for most of the world are men. 'God' is traditionally thought of as a masculine word. What female spiritual supreme being do women have to relate to? Mary is worshiped in some forms of Christianity, but not all. She is still a secondary figure to the masculine god, the masculine Christ.

Women have been traditionally sidelined in the language of all society. The word *woman* still refers to *man*, for *man* is embedded in the word *woman*. As does *person* which is based on the word *son*. The word *man* influences our views of our positions in chair*man*, chair*person*, *man*kind, fe*male*, post*man*, fire*man*. Male imagery is used in paper*boy*. We have always used the word *man* by itself to refer generically to both men and women. Our Canadian national anthem even refers to "all our *sons*' command"! The insidious effects of this language are not lost on many enlightened people in our society.

A young girl brought up in such language, even if enlightened parents point out to her the fallacy of the biased language regarding gender, takes such language into her being, into her heart, into her very perception of herself as a viable person in her society. Supportive and understanding parents, emphasizing her worth and goodness as a person, can do much to mitigate the thrust of society's insidious male-biased language. But the effect on her is still there: Her gender is not considered as important by the very language her society uses. Such negative language infuses my soul, any woman's soul. It contributes to a woman's repression of her force; it contributes to her **Inside suicide.**

ANCIENT GODDESS WORSHIP

Before Christianity, however, even before Judaism, there were peoples in the western European world, who believed the Female Deity supreme. In fact, there were many peoples throughout the world worshipping a female creatress. Merlin Stone in *When God Was a Woman* recounts her experience with this discovery: "Much to my surprise I discovered accounts of Sun Goddesses in the lands of Canaan, Anatolia, Arabia, and Australia, while the sun goddesses among the Eskimos, the Japanese, and the Khasis of India were accompanied by subordinate brothers who were symbolized as the moon." *(Stone, p. 2)*

*I per*sonally experienced a real shock when I also discovered the ability of people to worship a god as a female image. Twenty-five years ago, when I was at a church group of progressive women, one of the women led the group in a psalm praising God as a Woman, petitioning Her compassion and strength. My knees buckled with the thought. I felt weak. This idea felt wrong. I immediately identified the image with my mother, the woman in my family's home who had always had the secondary role to that of my Dad who was the strong one *because he was male*. He was the one I trusted with common sense; he was the one qualified to lead. He was after all, *the male*, and so the natural leader. The thought of my mother, and others like her, being born in the image of God, of a Goddess, was to me up-side-down, foreign beyond belief. But something in me led me to continue associating with this group of strong women. We study women's issues together. These friends are some of the strongest women leaders in our community, women who have set up homes for the disadvantaged, shelters and group homes for women and girls at risk. They raise money for women and people at risk in our country, and women in foreign countries as well. These women are incredible role models, winners of Peace Medals and Women of the Year Awards in our community. I love them dearly. But my introduction to the background of 'Goddess worship' was bumpy. I did not accept it quickly, or without question. It has taken me years. Now I immerse myself in the fantastic history of a culture of goddess worship basically lost to the modern world.

Riane Eisler, in *The Chalice and the Blade* explains historical Edens, peace-loving societies of thousands of years ago, thusly:

> We are all familiar with legends about an earlier, more harmonious and peaceful age. The Bible tells of a garden where woman and man lived in harmony with each other and nature - before a male god decreed that woman henceforth be subservient to man. The Chinese Tao Te Ching describes a time when the yin, or feminine principle was not yet ruled by the male principle, or yang, a time when the wisdom of the mother was still honored and followed above all. The ancient Greek poet Hesiod wrote of a "golden race" who tilled the soil in "peaceful ease" before a "lesser" race" brought in their god of war. (Eisler, The Chalice and the Blade p. xv)

Eisler's book expounds at length on this subject, which she prefigures in her introduction:

> Further verifying that there were ancient societies organized very differently from ours are the many inexplicable images of the Deity as female in art, myth, and even historical writings. Indeed, the idea of the universe as an all-giving Mother has survived, (albeit in modified form) into our time. Similarly, the veneration of Mary, the Mother of God, is widespread. Although in Catholic theology she is demoted to non-divine status, her divinity is implicitly recognized by her appellation Mother of God, as well as by the prayers of millions who daily seek her compassionate protection and solace. Moreover, the story of Jesus birth, death, and resurrection bears a striking resemblance to those of earlier "mystery cults" revolving around a divine Mother and her son, or, as in the worship of Demeter and Kore, her daughter. (Riane Eisler, p. xv)

THE SACRED FEMININE

Archeologists have found statues, icons and cave art dating back thousands and thousands of years, from the Paleolithic societies to the Neolithic societies of ancient Europe, statuettes found in archeological digs of female figures, statuettes which indicate a reverence for the female in society, proof of worship of the sacred feminine. Women were worshipped because they gave life, and nurtured that life. Archeologists and anthropologists conclude that there was no male dominance in these ancient societies. In more recent ancient history, from 6000 BCE to 2600 BCE, the island of Crete developed a highly developed society of peaceful civilization, one in which women, and the goddess were revered. This society, seemingly of equality between men and women, was gradually challenged, as the northern male-dominated warrior societies of the Kurgians, from 4300 BCE to 2800, began conquering southern European societies.

Eisler notes that "religion supports and perpetuates the society it reflects." (Eisler, p.67) This is indeed so, as we look at the religions extant in our own culture: Christianity, Islam, and Judaism. These male-dominated patriarchies reflect the idea of male dominance in our own society. Men are stronger physically, and considered the ones with the intelligence and opinions to be respected in our social situations. Women who do achieve respect have fought for their positions against the criticism of other women themselves who have learned to condone society's approval of men. Many women consider their secondary positions in society as the norm. One acquaintance proudly told me she has six grandsons! When I asked if she had any granddaughters, she said she has one granddaughter, currently in university. She was proud of this, but I had to ask! It is the grandsons who give her status in her community.

Merlin Stone explores qualities of the Goddess amongst various ancient peoples. In Strong and Garstangs's *Syrian Goddess* of 1913, in which some of the connections are explained. "Among the Babylonians and northern Semites She was Ishtar; She is Ashtoreth of the Bible and the Astarte of Phoenicia. In Syria her name was Athar, and in Cilicia it had the form of Ate (Atheh)." (Stone, p.22)

THE INSIDE SUICIDE: SHATTERING ILLUSIONS

In Robert Graves' translation of *The Golden Ass* by the Roman writer Apuleius of the second century AD, the goddess herself appears and explains:

> "I am Nature, the universal Mother, mistress of all elements, primordial child of time, sovereign of all things spiritual, queen of the dead, queen also of the immortals, the single manifestation of all gods and goddesses that are. My nod governs the shining heights of Heaven, the wholesome sea breezes, the lamentable silences of the world below. Though I am worshipped in many aspects, known by countless names, and propitiated with all manner of different rites, yet the whole round earth venerates me.
> The primeval Phrygians call me Pessinuntica, Mother of the gods; the Athenians sprung from their own soil, call me Cecropian Artemis; for the islanders of Cyprus I am Paphian Aphrodite, for the archers of Crete I am Dictynna; for the tri-lingual Sicilians, Stygian Proserpine; and for the Eleusinians their ancient Mother of Corn. Some know me as Juno, some as Bellona of the Battles; others as Rhamnubia, but both races of Aethiopians, whose lands the morning sun first shines upon, and the Egyptians who excel in ancient learning and worship me with ceremonies proper to my godhead, call me by my true name, namely Queen Isis. Ironically, Isis was the Greek translation for the Egyptian Goddess Au Set."
> (Stone, pp. 22-3)

Veneration of the Goddess in one form or other does seem to have dominated most of human history. I find it so lamentable that we have lost so much of this spirituality, this sense of the sacred oneness of the whole universe, the interconnectedness of the energies of its multitudinous parts. Riane Eisler expresses this sentiment also:

> Both the mythical and archeological evidence indicate that perhaps the most notable quality of the pre-dominator mind was its recognition of our oneness with all of nature, which lies at the heart of both the Neolithic and the Cretan worship of the Goddess. Increasingly, the work of modern ecologists indicates that this earlier quality of mind, in our times associated with some

types of Eastern spirituality, was far advanced beyond today's environmentally destructive ideology. (Eisler, p. 75.)

Many other modern spiritual writers note this deficiency in our modern culture, including Sue Monk Kidd in The Dance of the Dissident Daughter. "In Christianity there is a deeply embedded separation between spirit and nature ..... "(Kidd, p. 65) I find that those who are concerned deeply about our environment are among the most spiritually minded people in our society.

REPRESSION OF ANGER

Would that the world had continued with respect for the Sacred Feminine into a more balanced state of equal acceptance of the roles of men and women! Our emotions might have been more readily expressed, have been more honest. Anger: that emotion the church and modern patriarchal societies deny their people, especially their women. Good women do not erupt in anger, do not 'give in' to loud expressions of emotion, especially negative ones! Good women are accepting and understanding of what is going on, allow themselves to be programmed to suit others' needs! They become supersensitive to others' feelings and needs. Carolyn Heilbrun understands this: "If one is not permitted to express anger or even to recognize it within oneself, one is, by simple extension, refused both power and control. .... Forbidden anger, women could find no voice in which publicly to complain; they took refuge in depression or madness." (p. 13)

Sue Monk Kidd understands women's need to express anger:

The violation of women is an outrage, and anger is a clear and justifiable response to it. ...... Yet anger needs not only to be recognized and allowed; like grief, it needs to be transformed into an energy that serves compassion. ..... I had thought there were only two responses to anger: to deny it, or to strike out thoughtlessly. But other responses are possible. We can allow anger's enormous energy to lead us to acts of resistance against patriarchy. Anger can fuel our ability to challenge, to defy injustice. It can lead to creative projects, constructive behavior, acts that work toward inclusion. In such ways, anger becomes a dynamism of love. *(Kidd, pp. 74-5)*

A few years ago, one of my former teaching colleagues, whose husband had died a few months before, erupted in anger at another teacher, who was a very controlling person. My friend was not understood for her angry eruption; she was in fact highly criticized by many members of the staff. The group's sympathy instead went to the member who was the object of the anger. Good women are not supposed to 'erupt' in anger!

My colleague was expressing her grief through her anger, misplaced though it was at the time at another person. Many of her friends had predicted that she would have a breakdown, dissolving into months of tears and isolation when her husband died. When she didn't, she was regarded as still strong, the typical good woman, in complete control of herself, in charge of her emotions, able to give to, and be compassionate towards others. The natural manner in which she was expressing her grief, in anger, was not recognized as acceptable. Anger is one of the stages of grieving. The denial of her feelings over this incident has scarred my colleague. She is resilient. But the memory of the censure is still there. I feel so badly that this happened to her. Grief takes many natural stages and forms. But the emotion of anger, that important stage of grieving, is denied to women. Had my teacher friend found a more appropriate way to express her anger at her husband's death, it would not have built up to the point of explosion at other people; she would have been able to more appropriately express to the other person her disapproval of her actions. However, consideration that she might become angry at the devastating loss of her husband had not occurred to her as acceptable, as normal. We have all learned as children from church teachings and from societal acceptance of religious values that anger is bad. Anger is a natural emotion, and is often constructive.

GUILT

When justifiable anger is denied, it turns into feelings of guilt. This certainly has happened to me. When my mother died, I felt incredible anger at losing her. I remember the grief, and regret bordering on resentment, that I no longer had the loving support of a mother, as other girls did. I learned to cook, with brief advice from my father, and from mothers of my friends. I went looking for, and bought, a prom dress on my own. I missed my mother connection deeply. I learned to be self-reliant, probably standoffishly so. Even a wonderfully supportive father can supply only so much. Did I grieve? I wasn't allowed to. It would have hurt my dad more, already so deep in his own grief. I think now that I must have had feelings of anger at my mother for not being there to 'stay the course' for me. I know now that this is a natural phase of grief. Like my friend who lost her husband, I turned my anger into occasional outbursts of anger at other things, at other people. Misplaced anger. The targets of my anger always involved people who did not respect my needs, who ignored my feelings in some way. Some of my anger was justified. But the vehemence of it was excessive. I became very judgmental of people who were unable to respect my needs, and who appeared to ignore the needs of others. Yet I knew, even as a child, that anger was not a Christian or womanly virtue, so I tried to repress it. In my memory my mother became a paragon of virtue; she became untouchable in her perfection. Denied my anger and grief at her death, I gradually started to feel more and more guilt for her death; I hadn't been able to keep her alive. I wasn't good enough for her to stay well, to stay here taking care of us. The guilt became deep over the years, turning into a depression, a feeling of shame. My feeling of guilt deepened my shame of my own being. The real **Inside suicide!** A horrible result of repressed feelings!

THE CHURCH AS A FATHER-FIGURE

Even today, with all of the recent advances in society's attitudes toward women, many look to the Church for father-protection and father-figures. I experienced a wonderful feeling of parental protection as a child, a feeling which was extended by church values. Our church assumed the role of a father protecting children. Children do not disobey parents. Children trust. The church to which my family belonged exploited this. And since my own parent was the minister of the church, his position took on the powerful role for me of a guardian who was perfection itself, inseparable in role from the institution he worked for. Others thought of my father as better than most because he was 'the minister'. I adored him for this, putting him on a pedestal as better than anyone else's dad. And he was so well-educated; both his mind and reading were expansive. I had only to ask my paragon of a parent for any encyclopedic answer I wanted. He knew 'everything'! And in addition, his compassion for us and for those in his community seemed unbounded. He loved us, his daughter and son, with passion and adoration; he did as much as he possibly could for us, and with us.

I watch friends today adhere to church traditions and continue in church communities, because they essentially long for that wonderful sense of childhood protection the church promises: a Father who loves, who forgives, who enfolds, embraces and protects. The Promise of it all! You belong to 'our family'. God will take care of you! You don't have to struggle any more by yourself with the problems of life! If you join our church, we will take care of you! Such exclusivity! Many people become fanatically defensive of their religious beliefs. In fact, the church is the only place I know where I have to leave my mind at the door! And leave my autonomy outside also!

Robert J. Pirsig expresses the idea thusly. "When people are fanatically dedicated to political or religious faiths or any other kind of dogmas or goals, it's always because these dogmas or goals are in doubt." (Pirsig, p.134)

FAMILY PATTERNS

Women like me, indoctrinated by churches which have emphasized the role of the husband as head of the family, are taught from childhood to perceive the church's patriarchal energy as positive, not realizing that we ourselves as women are not living our lives fully as separate human beings, individual in thought and action, independent of the approval of men. The church has done our thinking for us, has taught us to close our minds, to rely on attitudes and values provided for us.

I realized as I searched for my identity, that much of my understanding of myself would come from discovering my own family roots. I have spent years delving, digging for these roots, helped by intensive therapy. In my family, my mother adored my father because he was a good man whose value system was inherent, the final word on Christian actions. Over the centuries, many women have moved from a house dominated by a father, whom they thought they had to please to a house dominated similarly by a husband, thinking of this as a naturally fulfilling existence. Many of my own friends married with this attitude. Carolyn Heilbrun raises this point about father-daughter relationships: "....the efforts of fathers to be accepted into the male world they do not question or challenge are vitally connected with their efforts to imprison their female children, however talented or encouraged, in the conventions of femininity." (pp. 69-70) This was certainly the unconscious attitude of my own father, despite his love and encouragement! I remember one of my mother's friends, years ago, saying that she used to get migraine headaches all the time, but that she hadn't had one since the day her husband died.

One of my former acquaintances, a university graduate, married a wonderful man who provided for his family extremely well; she raised two wonderful children with him. Now that he has died, she cherishes her independence so much that she has rejected men who are interested in her. She does not want to be the caregiver for another man. Many a woman has gone down the aisle on her wedding day, loving and trusting the partner waiting for her, but with a terrible, sinking feeling of dread. Not only did her father *give her away*, she was actually *giving herself away*! Like a sacrificial lamb. Heilbrun quotes Northrop Frye (ironically a contemporary and acquaintance of my father) on this: "The heroine who becomes a bride, and eventually, one assumes, a mother, on the last page of a romance, has accommodated herself to the cyclical movement: by her marriage . . . she completes the cycle and passes out of the story. We are given to understand that a happy and well-adjusted sexual life does not concern us as readers." (p. 86)   I did not marry until well into my thirties, knowing somehow instinctively that marriage in a subservient relationship was wrong for me. Subconsciously I was demanding the freedom I had not had while growing up, rejecting the restraints which male 'protection' provides. Heilbrun notes Anne Sexton's experience:

"Until I was twenty-eight I had a kind of buried self who didn't know she could do anything but make white sauce and diaper babies. I didn't know I had any creative depths. I was a victim of the American Dream, the bourgeois, middle-class dream. All I wanted was a little piece of life, to be married, have children. I thought the night-mares, the visions, the demons would go away if there was enough love to put them down. I was trying my damnedest to lead a conventional life. for that was how I   was brought up, and it was what my husband wanted of me. But one can't build little   white picket fences to keep nightmares out. The surface cracked when I was about twenty-eight. I had a psychotic breakdown and tried to kill myself". (Heilbrun, p.70).

    To be protected excessively often means giving up independence. Churches have promulgated the attitude that they are parent figures providing protection and approval, *as long as we leave our minds at the door!* I find this an insidious attitude depleting my ability to develop myself fully as a person! My autonomy is usurped! This has been paramount in creating my **Inside suicide.**

THE USE AND ABUSE OF WOMEN FOR COMPASSION IN LIFE

I have watched men also embrace the church in their need for a symbol of compassion, understanding, and intuition. I find this ironic, for these are qualities usually associated with women. Men have always turned to women's natures for support and understanding and sympathy in order to enhance their careers. Often I have found that men have depended on the women close to them to impart feminine energy to them so that they, the men, could gain compassionate strength to help them connect better with colleagues and friends. I have heard of male healers touching, actually physically feeling up, women who are in their trust, for the sole purpose of gaining feminine energy: an abuse of the women whom they are using for strength. One of my friends was at a healing circle, dancing by firelight, when the male leader of the retreat kept touching her, pawing her body. A form of sexual abuse. She realized that this was his attempt to garner her feminine energy for the work he was doing. Terribly uncomfortable, she left the retreat. As she was driving away, a snake crossed her path, the snake: a symbol of healing, a sign that she was doing the right thing in leaving, in listening to the intuition of her body. The best doctors and healers have a holistic approach to their practices, an approach that can only work well if intuition is included in understanding the total essence of the person being treated. Intuition, that gift of women. Men often tap their women for intuitive and healing strengths. This is wrong, if it is done without the consent of the woman, or if the woman is in a position of trust, or if the woman feels that she must comply out of a sense of duty, which occurs frequently with male doctors, lawyers, and clergy.

    Male clergy have often taken advantage of women's healing natures to help balance their masculine energies so that they can better access their own compassion and understanding. A few years ago, I was sitting near the back of the church at the funeral of a Roman Catholic woman teacher colleague, who had died of cancer. As the officiating priest went down the aisle to conduct this very difficult service, he touched the hand of a woman sitting on the aisle ahead of me, gathering strength. Who she was, I have no idea, but that she was able and willing to give of her own strength during her own sorrow, and that her bond with the priest was such that he could accept her strength, was so apparent to me. The role of the clergy requires them to dispense parental love and compassion to their parishioners, actions which help to fulfill their careers more successfully. But love and compassion cannot be dredged from a bottomless pit; these emotions need to be rejuvenated, replenished in order to continue blossoming. The clergy are considered better ministers if they are able to use compassion with sincerity; they themselves are better loved in return.

After my mother died of multiple sclerosis when I was sixteen, my father used me as a sounding board by confiding the problems of people in his congregation to me, gathering sympathetic energy from me. He also practiced his sermons on me. I was too young for this; I did not know how to protect myself from an authority figure that I loved, and who adored me as a daughter. As a result I was drained of my own strength at a time when I needed to grieve. I needed strength to develop as an independent and strong teenager, as a young woman in my own right. I was learning that supporting male figures was the way to succeed in life. I was proud of my ability to support my father in his 'sacred' career.

I realize now what a harmful and devastating effect illness has on a home. All family members' roles are skewed into the protection and care of the member who is ill. There is a lack of balance. My father needed to use me, in order to fulfill his role as a minister more completely. If the compassionate side of a man has been repressed because of what was expected of him as a male child, it is likely that he will turn to his women for support and confidence in order to perform better in his chosen profession. And what work does not require a man or woman to have human feelings? Men in careers like teaching and social work require understanding natures in order to be fully successful.

ROLES

Because women's natures are genetically provided with a sensitivity for connection, a need to mother others, we are easily exploited by people like ministers, priests, doctors, lawyers, and bosses. These jobs, and many others, are enhanced by feminine compassion. To allow loved ones and employers to rely on us so much that we are restricted in our own independent power, and thus are harmed from furthering our own abilities is wrong. How to know where to draw the line? A key question which institutions like the Church ignore. While I have been studying historical attitudes to men and women, I have come to the conclusion that the Christian church, which has had such a pervasive influence on the development of western society, is responsible for many of our attitudes and the roles we play in our lives. The church has enforced the idea that men are heads of households and that women are to serve men by providing background strength, both physical and emotional, to assist in forwarding *the men's* careers. Women's lives have been more confined to household tasks, to work which is closer to home-based activities. Men have been genetically programmed over the centuries to conquer. Sue Monk Kidd notes:

> As Jungian analyst June Singer points out, when a girl is growing up, it is not taken for granted as it is with boys, that her life and needs will be primary, that she will have access to places of authority and power like her brothers or father. What is taken for granted is that she will find her main source of fulfillment through her husband and family, that she will be secondary to them. .....When a woman lives out the Secondary Partner, she tends to believe, not so much consciously but deep inside, that she is there to be of service to her partner. (Kidd, p. 52)

I realize now how much I squelched my own opinions and attitudes, both in my family of birth, and in my marriage, in an effort to not be an 'uppity' woman, but a traditional docile woman who is loved for her sweetness and conformity to the family's needs and demands. We all fear rejection, need love, and work to attain approval; a primary response. Thankfully, my husband understands my need to do this work now of changing my attitudes, to correct the mistakes I have made in the past. Even if he didn't, I would have to keep going on my own course, of necessity. The journey, once started cannot be stopped. It forces me to let the real me gush forth.

In the last school in which I taught English, I suspect that I was hired as the Assistant English Head specifically because I was compliant enough as a woman to give the support to the male English Head. He needed to temper his hard-edged controlling attitude. Further, I realize that throughout my career, ideas which I sometimes presented in staff meetings which were rejected, were often adopted a year later when presented by male colleagues. I suspect that the sex of the person presenting and making the suggestions mattered.

Our mothers have colluded in this. Carolyn Heilbrun understands the psychology behind this drive:

> What was the function of mothers toward daughters before the current women's movement, before, let's say, 1970? Whatever the drawbacks, whatever the frustrations or satisfactions of the mother's life, her mission was to prepare her daughter to take her place in the patriarchal succession, that is to marry, to bear children (preferably sons), and to encourage her husband to succeed in the world. But for many women, mothers and daughters alike, there moved in their imaginations dreams of some other life: of personal accomplishment, of the understanding and control of hard facts and complex problems, of a place in a community where women were in sufficient numbers to render the accomplished woman neither lonely nor an anomaly. Above all, the taking control of one's life without the intrusion of a mother's patriarchal wishes for her daughter, without the danger of injuring the much loved and pitied mother. (Heilbrun, pp. 118-119)

My own mother became sick and died because she tried so hard to fulfill her role as a good wife under the patriarchal system into which she was born. I realize that her dreams of fulfillment in life, as an independent person were repressed with her marriage. Her subconscious anger must have been intense, the anger denied her as a 'good woman'. She certainly tried to raise me in the same spirit of subjection to the patriarchal system, of living to please the dominant male. Subconsciously, she must have questioned her role, for her dreams of creating art had become secondary once she married. I must have absorbed her subconscious desires; she must have imbued me with a latent spirit of rebellion.

Men learn the perception that they need to rule, be in charge, an attitude they have acquired from the society in which we live, an attitude instilled in our western society by Jewish and Christian traditions, an attitude which has infiltrated all aspects of our life. Again, Heilbrun sees clearly: "....in the Judeo/Christian tradition, manliness has been raised to an ideal perceived as warrior-like, free of the softer virtues of nurturance and affection. Men, who have defined themselves as *not* women, *not* their mothers have relegated the talents of intimacy to the female sex." (p.102)

THE MEANING OF PROTECTION OF WOMEN

It is not only Judeo/Christian society which has seeded this attitude; most religions seem to have been created on the premise of enhancing the positions of men. Muslim women are 'protected' even more than women in the western world, so much so that in some Muslim societies women's identities are obliterated as totally as possible by coverings like burquas when they leave the family home, and by strict societal rules governing the place of women in the home and in society. Muslim women are routinely beaten in their homes, a practice *condoned by law*, in order to subjugate them to second-class positions of servitude. Many Muslim societies condone the raping of wives. Ontario law condoned the raping of wives until 1983, when rape laws were broadened to include laws prohibiting the sexual assault of wives. In some parts of the world today, notably Afghanistan, women are still stoned for actions of *perceived* sexual impropriety. Men are sometimes stoned also, but less often, and with less cruelty than women: for women are buried in pits with their arms bound, while men are allowed the freedom of their arms to protect their heads as much as they can from this barbaric practice.

This is reminiscent of the western practice of burning and hanging witches, which began in the Middle Ages, and continued in rampant form right through the Seventeenth Century, into the Eighteenth! The last execution of a witch in England occurred in 1682. The last one in Europe occurred in Switzerland in 1782. The repeal of witchcraft laws as crime didn't occur in England until 1735. The Salem witchcraft trials in the United States occurred in 1692. Why did witchcraft become a crime to begin with? To subjugate people, to control them, to bend the populace to religious principles with fear. To stamp out individual thought. To stamp out any healing talents or creative feelings. Brutally!

In most religions only male clergy have been, and still are, the norm. Women have long been excluded from this profession which utilizes the natural attributes of women: intuition, sensitivity to others, compassion. The clergy becomes similar to an 'old boys club'. Many women still, even in Western society in this day, are not supposed to be able to think, to hold opinions of value separate from those of their partners! As a result of the male domination of the church hierarchy, much emphasis has been on church doctrine, to an extent that church doctrine has often been reduced to arguments and dictates about its fallibility and essential nature. Argumentation about doctrine is left-brained thought, as it utilizes the logical and reasoning part of the brain. Men's natures have relied on logical and competitive strategies in order to gain power. These attitudes lessen the impact of the essential message of Christianity of love and tolerance. Even if a particular denomination of Christianity has evolved to include a female ministry, as have many Protestant denominations, its basic beliefs still extol the male: the God, the Christ, the apostles, the prophets. Women were not, and still are not allowed, in most forms of religion, to develop their own heroines, to develop their own stories publicly. Women in the bible are always secondary figures. The books of both the Old Testament and the New are heavy in male imagery, in patriarchal figures. They are replete with the exploits and histories of men. The men are named: Adam, Moses, Abraham, David, Jesus, Peter, Saul and Paul. They are the heroes, and many more men like them. They have become the religious prophets who imparted 'the word of God'. What of their wives? What of prophetesses? Seldom are they mentioned, and even more seldom are they named. If they are, often, like Eve and Delilah, they are used as examples of what happens to women if they try to have influence above their stations, dragging down men with feminine 'inferior' perceptions of life. These are examples to men to of what can happen if a man relies on the opinions of his wife; they teach men to be careful of women's so-called inferior natures.

Much of the bible does indeed seem to be written to enhance male dominance, to keep women in their place. As a child it never occurred to me to question the proper 'nature of things', the place of women in society as inculcated in me by my parents and by the scriptures. Women followed men, obeyed their dictates, bowed to their superior opinions. If a woman was lucky, and chose well, she could find a gentle husband who treated her with respect, who didn't abuse her, who supported her both emotionally and financially. But at least when I was a young adult, we had the choice of whom to marry. Western society had progressed to that extent, even if we were still programmed to think of men as our superiors with the undisputed right to rule. While I have been reading extensively over my life, I have identified with the men in stories and history, not the women.

THE INSIDE SUICIDE: SHATTERING ILLUSIONS

Men are the ones who teach the value systems, who go out in the world, who have adventure and fun. Even today, when reading an article in a newspaper, for example, I often assume it to be written by a man; I still sometimes catch myself perceiving women as having little ability to give outspoken opinions.

PROGRAMMING

Often I am surprised when I look for the author of a newspaper article to find a woman's name. How we have been programmed! The June Callwoods of the world were people I have admired, but have not really understood. How have they ever found the strength to express themselves! Their upbringings must have been so different than mine. It has taken me most of my life to find my voice! The damage we do to children; still do!

I perceive clearly now that this unbalanced system, which has developed over centuries and centuries, has given our society the attitude that men have the right to judge us as women, that men exist for the purpose of judging and controlling women, and are perfect in their abilities to do so simply because they are men. Men, endorsed by churches as heads of households, have sought women who are tractable as helpmates, "sweet in nature"; women who obey easily, and yet at the same time are compassionate and affectionate. My own mother was beautiful and pious, two qualities that were enough for my Dad to fall in love. My stepmother, while still playing the secondary role, had a little more common sense in making decisions, in her ability to feel independent in her marriage. Nevertheless, most women have been raised in this pattern of supplying support, taught to mold themselves into the personalities of good potential wives. While both my mother and my stepmother were loving compassionate women, their primary consideration in life was supporting my father in his career without question.

Women have come to be considered beautiful if they are docile, obedient, and sympathetic to others' problems. Be sweet! Forgive! Be understanding! Support! Doing only this depletes a woman's potential ability to fulfill herself to the utmost in her life, to view herself as an independent entity. It squelches *her own* voice. Her potential to succeed as an individual has been ignored and demeaned in so much of our society. I was fortunate to have a father who encouraged me to get an education, despite his subconscious need to keep me in a secondary supportive position. Many women today in the western world do have the opportunity to break from the traditional patterns of social gender roles, and if they have been lucky, they have had strong mother figures who have not only encouraged their daughters in their self-fulfilling goals, but have been role models themselves of independence. Our society is changing, but slowly.

I was expected, by both of my parents, to become like my mother, in fact to become her. While I did fight against this as a child, once my mother became ill, I actually *became* her, identifying with her grief and suffering. I tried very hard to keep her alive. I needed her to be alive. She had fought so valiantly to live. She needed me to understand her, to identify with her struggle her in her desperate drive to live. I needed to understand her needs as fully as possible in order to take care of her before and during her long illness. Caregivers lose a sense of themselves as individuals. Caring for my mother, and to a good extent for my family, was very difficult for me as a teenager attending school. I lost myself, literally. I longed for the mother I didn't have. I was expected by my family automatically to do the things I did. I expected these actions of myself. The good, good daughter. The selfless daughter. And indeed I tried to make myself unselfish, and as a result became truly 'selfless'. Ironically, I hated my mother for her weakness, for her seeming abandonment of me while I pushed to keep her alive. When she died, we did not express our grief openly. It was too painful to have to watch each other grieving the physical and mental devastation, the loss of our beautiful mother and wife. My Dad said to me before the funeral, "Now you be a soldier!" So I gradually learned to suppress my grief, primarily for him, for it would have shocked us both to express it. And so my justifiable anger gradually turned into guilt. My anger was essentially denied by church attitudes and conventions. It was forbidden. I became warped in my views of myself, as I repressed and changed my memories of my mother. **My inside suicide.**

I see clearly now that my mother, while she loved my father passionately, lost herself when she married. Before her marriage, she had a good degree of independence, working in my grandfather's photographic studio as an artist. She did much independent painting herself, as well. Beautiful oils and watercolors. Beautiful china designs, and hand painting. But after marriage, her essential creative being dissolved in the expectations placed on her of keeping the household for my father, of being the minister's perfect wife, which in those days required a lot of actual work and support in a church. Churches essentially hired two for the price of one. She always felt inadequate, not perfect enough, not educated enough. I think she became ill because she lost herself. **Her inside suicide.**

∞

EDUCATIONAL BACKGROUND

While I was encouraged to go to university, expected to, in fact, for my father was proud of an educated daughter, I was still expected to fulfill the secondary role of a woman in my society. My Dad felt that if I was educated, I could protect myself from disaster if my marriage fell apart with illness or death. It was assumed that my independence was revoked the moment I married. What a quandary! We as women have spent so much of history being made into innocent victims, feeling responsible for the egos of others who are using our female energy to enhance themselves. Thus our society, by accepting male dominance and superiority, has endorsed a very real form of unconscious emotional rape of our women. This has had devastating effects on my own sense of self-confidence, on my ability to think of myself as a worthwhile being. Helping someone else fulfill his career is not self-fulfilling, self-energizing. That's what I did as a child and young adult. I supported my Dad's emotional needs, as well as my mother's. I succeeded well at school to please my Dad. I listened to my Dad's problems and perceptions of his job as a minister because I wanted his love, because I thought that was my responsibility, my duty, because I perceived a kind of power in doing so. But it was not self-fulfilling power. My own interests and abilities were encouraged to a limited extent only, within the boundaries of academic learning, within the boundaries of church thinking and religious society. My own life achievements and creativity were squelched in my early years. My mother was trying to mold me into the role of being a good, docile Christian daughter, one who knows her place, who is well-trained to support a husband. Like other girls, I was taught to repress my more risk-taking nature, my assertiveness, for these qualities were not ones which would please the men I knew or wanted to attract. I really was not encouraged to think for myself about life's big issues, to become my own person, to explore my own interests. Life was precarious. Protect yourself, Daughter!

As I developed in my career as a teacher, I saw girls growing into womanhood with feelings of inferiority regarding their own intelligence and social power, of which I instinctively did my best to be aware, and help correct as far as I could. Yet I still felt very fragile about my ability to shape and influence the departments and schools in which I worked. While I knew I was clever, and held valid opinions, I did not trust my voice in speaking up in staff meetings for school organizational issues about which I was passionate. Other more confident teachers could easily put me down. As a result, I was sometimes bitter about my ability to feel success in my teaching positions. I know now, from things I have been told by parents and students and other teachers that I underestimated my effects on my students and staff. It's all a matter of being allowed to be oneself. Of learning how to be oneself within the dictates of the system. I lament that I was often not strong enough to be myself.

Ye the more I taught, the more I realized the absolute importance of education in giving young people the confidence to challenge ideas and accepted norms in society. This confidence of learning background enables people to break from confining traditions, while at the same time, giving them the tools to learn to discern which societal requirements are necessary for them to live within their lives.

∞

SEXUAL REPRESSION

Widely accepted ideas of sexual attractiveness play a large role for women. A double standard is created for us, especially within church communities. We were taught by social convention that we must be attractive physically, but not sexually. Churches have tended to compound the harm done to women's psyches by implying that women who are attractive *sexually* will not be regarded by men as wholesome, loving, pure partners. I have watched over the years how women within church societies have struggled to be physically attractive, without being sexual; I realize that I have striven for this image for most of my life. I watched my mother and my stepmother do the same, and my aunts, my friends, their mothers and our grandmothers. Church tradition emphasizes propriety to the point of making women hypocritical. Too much display of sexual initiation is considered aggressive in behaviour, even immoral. In mating, men have seemingly always had the superior position of judging and choosing. Attitudes of sexual behaviour were passed on to me from my mother. I was taught that repressing my sexuality was the way a decorous girl, a 'good' girl, succeeds, and is accepted by society. I was taught by both parents to guard my virginity above all else, not only for my own reputation, but for the reputation of my family. My family's place in society would be compromised if my virginity had been compromised, either by my own actions, or even by rape. Guard yourself, Daughter! Such a responsibility for a young woman! Many families have been changed forever, destroyed, by the physical violation of a daughter, and the family's acceptance of the accompanying shame. Attitudes today in western society are not as stringent, but are still adhered to, and even enforced in many communities, especially in strict religious societies. These attitudes make it difficult for a woman to express herself and her personality freely!

Religious mores often teach that sexual fulfillment for anything but direct procreation is sinful. The church has evolved over the centuries into a master of shame and guilt, when it comes to teachings about the physical body. The beauty of my body, of my natural sexual movement, of my sexual pride, was usurped by my family and my religious community. I learned as a young woman to hold myself stiffly when I moved, when I walked, especially when I was in the church. I learned to repress any free movements, to try not to be flirtatious or overtly sexual. Women like me lose their identities in 'playing the game'. We actually kill off the part of ourselves that shows expression of joy. We commit suicide emotionally! **An inside suicide!** Because of my inability to be myself, and the necessity of identifying with the needs of my mother, my family, my society, I subconsciously developed a feeling of falseness about myself because of what my parents and society expected of me. I often felt 'dirty'. I developed a very real sense of emotional rape similar to the feelings of women who have been actually physically raped. When I read Joyce Carol Oates' *We Were the Mulvaneys*, I identified to such an extent with the daughter who had been raped that I wondered if I had sustained an actual physical assault, which I was repressing. Through therapy I discovered that the assault I sustained was an emotional one, just as damaging. I used to have feelings of worthlessness, powerlessness, helplessness. Women like me become angry if we feel 'used' in any way. I developed wooden feelings and wooden actions as I responded to society's demands of 'duty'. I tried to repress my anger, which later erupted as judgment of others' actions. If I don't feel beautiful as a woman, or have the right to be physically attractive, I am unable to be my true self. I am still trying hard to reclaim myself from the confining view that patriarchal religious institutions have thrust upon me.

    The most basic creative force which we as human beings have is our sexual energy, the vibrant life force. Sexual activity inspires good art. I see repression of sexual enjoyment by the church as akin to rape, for such repression takes away a person's sense of self. If sex is thought of as wrong, or even as something to be severely restricted, then even thinking sexual thoughts makes people feel wrong about themselves. But sexual thoughts are impossible to repress. We are human beings, not perfect! We are born with sexual natures. A culture which endorses keeping a woman 'pure' strips her of her sexual feelings, of her individuality. It implies ownership of her by others. It obliterates her sexual beauty. The Judeo/Christian tradition has attached strings to sex, making it conditional. I am not advocating free sex. We do need to approach sexual encounters with responsibility. But the idea of a woman being considered 'spoiled', 'damaged goods', if she has sex outside of a traditional marriage, even by rape, is nonsense. Women are not property. We need to be able to feel responsibility for our own bodies, for our own sexual activities.

∞

THE DOUBLE STANDARD

A repressive attitude to sex affects men as well as women, for men can become afraid of their own sexuality also, of their natural feelings for their bodies, and become afraid of women as a result. Men often feel guilty for admiring the beauty of the female body, a feeling which is subverted into undercover 'dirty jokes' with the 'boys'. Many men repress their sexual prowess by aligning themselves with socially acceptable wives; many lead double lives in order to find sexual fulfillment: an obvious double standard. I have seen male friends and acquaintances relegate their women into two categories: the ones to marry, and the ones with whom to have sex. Such an unnatural and potentially harmful way to live! The women in the lives of such men often suffer greatly, as well as the men themselves. How many marriages have been ruined by unfaithful partners, who love their spouses, but are enticed by the forbidden thrill of sex outside marriage? Marriages succeed best if partners are faithful, certainly! But the problem arises if one partner marries an image of what a good partner should be, in order to have social standing. Life is fulfilling when lived with honesty and awareness.

We have been taught by many segments of our society that women are so precious that they must be hidden, modest, while at the same time they are viewed as failures if they do not attract men. We have been taught that we are valuable to society mainly as wives and mothers in marriage, valuable for procreation. We take the blame if our society descends into debauchery. Men's urges are labeled as 'natural'; women's are 'controllable'. Therefore, women are considered the guardians of societal sexual mores, and responsible if these mores go awry. What nonsense! This is why invading armies rape the women of the conquered country in warfare: to try to destroy the home life and trust of the central values of the society. I believe that this double standard regarding the value of women, which religious institutions have endorsed, and in fact, promulgated, has affected men and women alike to a terribly negative extent. All of us have the right to develop our own bodies and spirits freely, free of sexual oppression, free of biased and judgmental views. Only when we break free of repressive views can we accept ourselves as equals in society. Only when we break free of our own repressive views of ourselves can we respect ourselves well enough to fulfill our lives according to *our own* needs. Only then can men and women accept, and enjoy each other as equals.

∞

THE INDOCTRINATION OF PERFECTION

When I was growing up I felt quite inadequate, gradually becoming narrower and narrower in my interpretation of life, in my ability to take on new risks. I became more and more afraid of making mistakes, of not living up to the expectations men had of me. At a fortieth wedding anniversary reunion we attended recently, our longtime friends told the story of going on a picnic with the husband's visiting mother, soon after they were first married. The young wife forgot the sandwiches on which she had spent so much careful time. She was able to laugh at the situation, instead of feeling ashamed. Her husband, initially angry, respected her attitude, and ability to adapt to unexpected situations. As I listened to the story, I had increasing respect for my childhood friend, for not accepting her husband's criticism, and I gained respect for him in that he accepted her as imperfect, and loved her for it. Why has our society developed the idea that women must be perfect, able to do all things? I think that this has come from the pervasive idea that Christianity represents the ultimate spiritual union for which people strive in life. Perfection. Christianity, viewing itself as perfect, has spawned the conception that it is *the truth. The One and Only Truth!* This religious system is based on ancient Greek ideals of pure love, perfect caring. Hence, miracles, perfect healing. Perfect women. So we women are still often revered by men as long as we aid and abet the male vision. In doing so, we neglect our own visions. This happened to me as a young woman. I had no faith in my own visions, in my own power. I had difficulty viewing myself as able to influence the world positively, as able to make a difference.

As a child and young woman, I constantly watched as women fawned over my Dad, the minister. It was safe for them to flirt with this forbidden man, for he was protected by his position. He was considered so good that he would never take advantage of their attractions. Clergy in the church have been thought of as perfect in themselves. Many people see the minister as an extension of God Himself. Many ministers themselves actually come to think of themselves in this way. Women ministers thus present problems for many more traditional thinkers in church societies, and are often not considered acceptable. They don't fit the image! Many male ministers have taken the adoration of their women parishioners to heart, and subconsciously accepted the attitude that they must indeed be perfect. I saw this misguided perception in ministers who came into our home as guests. As a child, I accepted it completely. The minister becomes a sexual object analogous to 'forbidden fruit', connected to sex as God the Tease, The Apple. I saw this so often in the attitudes of women to my father. It is very obvious that problems can arise over this, as many clergymen have found out! I think this problem is probably more prevalent in Protestant communities than in Catholic ones in which clergy do not marry; the very ability of a minister to marry, have children, indicates that he is indeed a real sexual being, while Catholic clergy, who do not marry, have traditionally been perceived as asexual creatures. But everyone has natural, normal sexual urges, whether or not they have invoked vows of celibacy, as have the clergy of the Catholic church. Problems arise either way both for clergy, and for their parishioners.

Many Roman Catholic clergy have invited trouble, and tainted the image of The Church. Imagine what it must be like to have taken a vow of celibacy, and to find oneself impure because one still has sexual urges. A friend of mine, a former Roman Catholic priest, who had left the priesthood, confided in me that he had to leave the religious life because he couldn't repress his sexual urges after he had taken his vows. He never acted on his sexual urges; just felt them still there. He deemed himself unclean, unworthy of his position, because he would 'lust after women' whom he saw walking down the street. He felt that he should be able to repress his urges totally, negate them in his body, if he was to be pure enough to hold his religious title within The Church. He believed that he was supposed, to be 'pure', a robot, not human.

Consider the multiple cases of the Catholic clergy who have abused young boys within their influence. The ones that we know about. Parents sent their young boys to church to be choir boys, to be close to the 'good' influence of the priests. The shock, the betrayal by the priest who abuses his power, must be overwhelming for those who experience the abuse! Children trust those who care for them. Who is in a better position to command total respect than a Catholic priest over children? So why have priests abused their power so abominably in a sexual way with young boys? My theory is that it is of course impossible for anyone as a human being to repress the basic sexual urge, the life force. But churches have traditionally taught that women are basically impure because they tempt men simply by 'being'. Therefore, to alleviate the feeling of sexual need, the basic human urge, male priests have turned to boys as a source of relief, boys whom they could terrify into silence with threats of breaking vows of confidentiality. Secrets! The bane of healthy social function! The priests believed, falsely, that the young boys would 'get over' any anguish they felt, that it was not really harmful to them, that they were serving a useful and good function in serving the 'men of God'! The clergyman as an image of perfection!

Because the clergyman has the role of human perfection in the pulpit, a parishioner can feel that the priest or minister is preaching directly at *him or her, into one's very soul,* knowing what is in one's imperfect thoughts and actions. I certainly felt this, even though the preacher was my own loving and understanding father, for he preached into *my heart!* I sat there feeling wooden, pierced through, and dead. **My inside suicide.** In addition I worried in case my father said something controversial for which he would be criticized. I took into my own being the fear that I myself would be criticized for saying something controversial. Such misconceptions repressed my own spiritual being to a tremendous extent, fostering a sense in me of not being good enough, of intense claustrophobia. I recently heard a psychologist being interviewed on the radio, who was saying that claustrophobic feelings are common in churches, and that many people actually faint from the feelings. We feel we have to be perfect, perfect for our church, for our parents, for our families. No wonder we feel we have to be perfect for our children. Raise perfect children. Idealism taken to extremes! No wonder church adherents feel dreadfully ashamed if things go wrong for them in their families. We automatically take our imperfections to heart, feel shame, and blame ourselves for problems which inevitably arise in our lives. Often we feel that we are loved by our parents only if we live up to their expectations as authority figures; we feel we are loved *conditionally.* Idealism carried by religious expectations to such an extreme in its expectations of perfection is a serious, frightening, and harming weakness.

THE ROLE OF SHAMING IN CONTROL

This need for perfection which has been such a central pivotal point of church teachings, has led to additional very twisted and sobering consequences. If a person is to be as perfect as possible, the person must strive for self-abnegation in totality, for by our very human, physical natures, we are necessarily imperfect. Yet it is apparent to me that every physical thing on our planet has beauty by its very uniqueness. None can be perfect in comparison with another. By advocating self-abnegation in an effort to achieve perfection, the church has developed the theory of sin, thus canceling the beauty of individuality, thus setting up people to judge others. Church systems have become so judgmental! This system separates me from my higher self, from my Godliness. It makes me feel incredibly guilty if I feel that I cannot please, that I cannot achieve the standard well enough, that I am flawed. I know that this led me to become intensely self-conscious. In requiring perfection, the church has become adept in its ability to make people like me feel shame for my actions, for my trials and errors in life.

Women particularly have been harmed by controlling patriarchs. We became ashamed of our bodies, which certainly do attract men. Thousands of years ago, in religions like Judaism, male clergy, afraid of their own sexuality, as impure, made women objects of shame, simply because they were women. The sweetness of sexual feeling was therefore forbidden as shameful, and thus the very sweetness of love became forbidden. This tradition has continued under the guise of modesty. Thinking of things sexual as evil has warped many people. For example, influenced so strongly by my Christian tradition, I became afraid of normal contacts with people of the opposite sex, afraid of normal situations like flirting. As a teenager I was definitely attracted to boys, but felt that contact with them was somehow wrong, dirty. I knew that dating and sex were normal parts of life. My friends took part in them. But I somehow felt wrong in dating, in alien territory! Young women raised in church traditions can learn to feel innately afraid of being admired physically by others, even afraid of talking to someone of the opposite sex, because they feel guilt at experiencing the normal human energy of attraction even in a simple conversation. Childhood practices and beliefs become ingrained to such an invasive, and often harmful, extent. The feeling of violation of myself by the *examination* which I felt from the church was an incredible invasion of my privacy! I was continually trying to please! Violation is anything which violates the *person*, emotionally, physically, spiritually.

    I feel that shaming someone, as my parents and church did to me when I was young, has had further consequences. It is really an attempt to prevent the other person, so often a child, from embarrassing the adult figure who is doing the shaming. Shaming is a way of controlling others. The image is that our family must look perfect. Since my family and I were conditioned by church society to feel morally superior, as the *first family*, as examples, any imperfections I perceived in myself I felt to be moral deformities in my character, in my essential being. This made me feel inferior, not good enough for union with the Divine; and not good enough for a relationship with a man; that is, not good enough to find the Divine within myself, and therefore not good enough to take my place in the world. Shaming conquers love of self, respect for self.

    In no way am I advocating a life lived so freely and selfishly that it is devoid of responsibility. A life well-lived definitely involves a sense of responsibility to others, of responsibility to community. Living with honesty to ourselves and others, is an absolute basis before a life of fulfillment can be achieved. This sense of responsibility begins first and foremost with a sense of responsibility to one's *self*, a pride in self which leads to confidence. It is when social institutions like the church impose responsibility with guilt, inflicted either emotionally or physically, that the self is damaged.

∞

THE HARM OF JUDGMENTAL ATTITUDES

In an effort to respond to the Church's judgment on scales of perfection, many women like me adopt a sense of duty to our families and communities. We try to fit into the ideal of 'the good woman' by doing the expected womanly actions of showing compassion, giving to others, caring for others. I went into teaching partly to fulfill my need to help others. Deeds which are useful to society make us feel at peace with ourselves according to what society encourages and admires. There is so much good that the church does for society. But problems arise for the 'do-gooder' when she starts to perceive of herself as righteous because of her deeds, as morally better than others whom she is helping. I have watched myself and my friends fall into this trap. Doing good deeds gives one a real 'ego trip'. I know of few who are able to do good deeds without falling into the trap of becoming identified with their deeds. I admire greatly those who can dissociate from the image of the do-gooder.

As we try to help those in the world with fewer advantages than we have, some of us ignore the heart-wrenching plights of those closest to home. By distancing themselves physically in the good deeds they perform, many women are able to distance themselves from the emotional drain on them which compassion for others causes. How does one care, have compassion, yet still maintain one's centre? To give with perfection is to give until burnout, something many people experience in life. In my career I gave as much as my sensitive body would stand, to the point of burnout, and illness. I am paying now with physical pain for my lack of perspective on my life.

To express myself effectively in life, I have had to accept myself as imperfect. I have had to accept that while some will love me for who I am, some will criticize, and others will even reject me totally. I cannot please everyone. No one can please everyone! Yet my imperfection is contrary to the expectations of church teachings. If a woman like me tries to be obedient to the idea of perfection, inculcated in her from childhood, self-expression becomes almost impossible. I will commit an error somewhere. Someone will disapprove. I will judge myself harshly, perceiving myself as having a 'fault'. I learned to fear myself, retreat into myself in depression. I am learning now that, if I express my own feelings from my heart about a subject, that I am stating what is right for me in my life. If others understand me, they will respect my views, and not judge me because I have views which may be different.

When I was in church, I felt part of an exclusive club of people with feelings of superiority, often masked as tolerance for other societies, races, religions, churches. We considered that the Roman Catholics down the street were 'good people' who were misguided. My Dad was very proud of his friendship and association with the Jewish rabbi and his family, but these were definitely people who were 'different', who deserved our sympathy and understanding because of the horrors and deprivations they had been through especially during the Second World War. But we were luckier because we were Christian. My family was very judgmental in its tolerance.

The following is a story that I find absolutely horrifying in its judgment. Friends of ours, who had supported the local Anglican church in town, were worried because their grandchildren had not been baptized. Their daughter and her partner did not attend church. The couple approached their Anglican rector, and asked about the possibility of having their grandchildren baptized. The rector refused them the rite of formal baptism on the grounds that their daughter and her partner were not officially married, nor members of the church. Instead the rector offered to 'bless' their grandchildren on the same Sunday, and in the same ceremony as the one in which members' pets were 'blessed'. The grandchildren were reduced in the eyes of the rector, and of the church, to the level of four-legged animals! They were not considered as human, because they had been born 'out of wedlock'! This judgment appalls me! Our friends were deeply hurt! The husband of our friends responded to his wife's distress for her grandchildren by bringing the family together in their own home one Sunday, and baptizing the children himself. I love him for this! His understanding of the judgment and exclusivity of the church! His compassion for his wife's distress! This couple has had no dealings with any church since. They learned the hard and painful way what some churches really are about: hypocrisy.

The need for perfection has led to judgmental attitudes of people who are different. By trying to become perfect and live the best life possible, we have narrowed our abilities to see others clearly, to see our relationship to others as equal. We become elitist. Recently, when I went into the local United Church office to donate to a cause, I heard one secretary tell the other that this donation was 'off the street'. I was highly offended by the implied exclusion, by the implied judgment of my lack of belonging. As a result I questioned within myself my own feeling of superiority in being able to donate a little to a part of the world which was suffering. And I realized that *understanding* for those who are different is a demeaning attitude if there is not total *acceptance* of people who are living as their circumstances require. Understanding and compassion are different than acceptance. I catch myself being judgmental, even though I have thought this problem through for years. The reaction from childhood is automatic. There can be no global perspective of other races and religions in a 'we/they' mentality, for 'they' are still different. Throughout history the church has so often fomented violence in the name of religion, and parts of the church are still doing so today. I think that judgmental attitudes breed intolerance with their emphasis on what we *should* say, *should* act like. "Should" ideas set us up to be judgmental of other people; we expect others to act according to our own standards of how we think they *should* act, instead of accepting others for living their lives in ways that they see fit.

Further, this judgmental Christian model of perfection implies the perfection of *men* simply by birthright. This concept of the superiority of men inflicted an inherent feeling of shame on me as a woman, for I was by definition defective. I learned to consider myself as morally unequal to men, not just physically unequal. Men were the ones to decide on the correctness of actions. They were the ones with practical common sense.

Yet paradoxically, young women like me brought up within the pale of church thought, were taught that many men were potentially dangerous, violent, insensitive, and aggressive, especially if they did not come from church communities, where presumably they had been taught the gentle art of sensitivity. Churchgoing men were considered safer, more thoughtful, and therefore more likely to treat a woman well. Be careful, Daughter, whom you choose as a partner, for the man is in charge of relationships within the home. His ideas rule! Women are considered to be basically inferior!

RIGHTEOUSNESS

Often religious righteousness is used to subtly indoctrinate children. My parents, usually my mother, often told me how lucky I was to be brought up in a Christian family. I became judgmental, thinking myself better than others. Yet simultaneously I was beset by doubts about my own abilities to live up to standards which my parents had set for me. The young mind cannot distinguish conflicting attitudes. Children simply absorb the ideas that something is wrong with the adult's ideas. They still try very hard to adjust their own little minds to fit those of the adults, for children need to please in order to receive love and nurturing. Protecting children too much is harmful if the protection controls what children learn, and how they act. Children need to be guided so that they learn not to harm themselves, or others. They will develop their own personalities, discover at their own rates, and learn to find their own ways in society, without the interference of adult judgment. They learn by example more than in any other way. School boards who ban the works of phenomenal authors like Margaret Lawrence, because there are very occasional and brief references to sexual acts, do their students a great disservice. Teenagers are able to analyze: to distinguish between attitudes to life that they want to adopt or reject. Children protected obsessively until they are adults do not learn to fit into society well. They do not trust their own decisions as adults. They become hesitant, and lack common sense.

Ingrained attitudes such as these have caused many psychological problems for me. From the righteous judgments my family and society made about me, I became extremely judgmental toward myself without even being aware of it. I felt greatly inferior. I would put myself down in conversations. I seldom spoke up for my ideas. If I felt disapproval from elders, I felt that I was the one at fault, that I was a failure for not fitting in. I did not trust my own ideas. When I felt unappreciated, I strove even harder for perfection. Often I became a workaholic. I still often blame myself if others do not accept my opinions or views. I feel responsible for others' feelings. I think that there is no more potent form of censorship than the fear of hurting others.

Charles Darwin was terrified of publishing his *Origin of Species*, for he knew how many people it would offend. Fortunately his scientific friends realized its importance, publishing it for him. Some of the friends of Darwin and his wife did reject them, offended at Darwin's opposition to the traditional views of organized religion. Many were scandalized. Darwin, extremely hurt by this criticism and rejection, felt deep guilt for the hurt he caused others. He felt isolation. Fears of creating feelings like these have kept me in my shell, afraid of my power if I spoke out. I found that in the schools in which I taught, I was often regarded as a trouble maker. I learned to try to keep my ideas to myself. I'm so sorry I did this! But to be outspoken, I had to be willing to accept the consequences. Heilbrun, quoting Patricia Spanks, points out, "The face a man turns to the world . . . typically embodies his strength', while the only acceptable models for women *"involve deception and yielding,"*. (Spanks, 1976, 59) (p. 22)

    As a result of fearing righteous reprisal, I learned a lack of trust in others. I developed a sense of claustrophobia as I allowed my soul to become more and more repressed by society and by my own self-judgment. I developed hypersensitivity to the needs of others. I developed a subconscious sense of falseness about the attitudes of society, which deeply affected my attitude to myself and to others. I have friends who adhere to church society even though they acknowledge the harm the same church teachings have created, and still create. I wonder at the harm such denial must be creating in their own beings, as it has in mine. To adhere to tenets in which you do not really believe, mainly for social reasons, is to live a lie. Yet I realize that to many people, identity with church society is self-identity; to leave would be to have no longer a sense of one's own person. I have lived through this torment, and am still doing so. The guilt I feel at no longer belonging, being within the pale, is often intense. But the guilt I would feel by returning to a society I know is deeply wrong for me would cause me such anguish that I could no longer live with myself. To live an untruth leads to deep depression, which I have experienced. To live like this affects one's health adversely. It has affected mine. I have developed environmental illness, and now rheumatoid arthritis. I know now why these diseases have surfaced in my body.

∞

USING RELIGION TO PROTECT

To justify our own beliefs and practices, we become righteously judgmental of other people's religions, of other people's customs, of their races. We seek to protect ourselves from ideas which are too different, too difficult to handle. But making those different from us into demons leads to polarization of races and religions. It leads to wars. To terrorism. To reprisals. To such incredible loss, suffering, deaths in our fragile societies.

To protect the family with religion, parents learn to mold their children into good adherents of the faith. The idea of breaking a daughter's spirit in order to mold her into a good Christian Daughter is so outrageous, so damaging! This certainly was my parents' attitude to bringing me up. In contrast, my brother had this attitude applied to him minimally. My parents applied this theory to me because it was applied in their homes, because it had been passed on from generation to generation as the way to bring up a daughter. Boys had different standards applied to them. To 'break a daughter's spirit', one teaches her to walk decorously as a young girl, not run; one teaches her to laugh softly, not boisterously; one teaches her to sit with her legs together, to be modest; one teaches her to be aware of everyone else's feelings, especially those of men, and to defer to them. You spank her to 'keep her in line', if necessary. You teach her to be quiet, to keep her thoughts to herself, lest she offend, lest she impose herself too much into the conversation. You teach her what her 'place' in her society is, and will be. Of course, you take her to church to enforce the traditions of thousands of years of social policies handed down through church teachings, of women being punished by society for stepping out of their places.

I have a Baptist friend who, having been through a painful divorce, purposely keeps herself too heavy, unattractive in dress and appearance, so that she will not have to deal with interested men. She thinks, 'Why should I give up the freedom I have, in order to defer to and take care of another man for the rest of my life?' In order to remain in the society in which she was raised, she has had to compromise her life force, her sexual joy, her instinctive need for companionship. I feel for her.

"Safety and closure, which have always been held out to women as the ideals of feminine destiny, are not places of adventure, or experience, or life. .... They forbid life." (Heilbrun, p. 20)

∞

SOCIETAL CONTROL

From the reading I have done over the years, and from what I have seen in my society, I realize that the church has adopted these attitudes in order to control the lives of its parishioners. There seems to be an authoritarian formality in the way the church disseminates its message. In most denominations a fairly narrow group of simple rules for life are given to the flock. As a result church adherents often dictate to others on actions which go way beyond the moral, into the area of manners. Sometimes this becomes ridiculous, including things like etiquette for dining. Recently, we were at a party where the hostess explained at the end, when we were helping wash up, that the women at her church declared that every piece of flatware and silverware on the table, whether used or not, had to be washed. I also was taught this by my mother. Women in social church circles have to know the behavioral rules for acceptance into society. Because this dictum about silverware washing had come from *church women*, it had more power over our friend. She was not able to use her own common sense in deciding whether utensils required washing. Even from this seemingly trivial example we can see that we are taught how we and others *should* act in situations of implied religious morality. This leads to an amazing loss of freedom for us, creates such inhibition about so many aspects of our lives, all in a desire for inclusion, for social acceptance. Correctness leads to morality. Pleasing God leads to feeling restricted, or sinful, controlled by threats.

In such a repressive atmosphere, passed on from mother to daughter and granddaughter, we teach our children that they are being selfish if they indicate their own needs. Instilling feelings of guilt in children, telling them that they are sinful or selfish if they do not think of the needs of others first, is an easy and effective method of control, of achieving politeness and obedience. But at what cost? Our children literally have 'The Fear of God' instilled in them.

'The fear of being defective': My parents did this to me extensively in their efforts to raise a good daughter. If I did something 'out of line', out of the expected norm, I was asked, "What's the matter with you?", implying a basic fault in my nature. This parenting technique is an incredible violation of spirit, of individuality, of the right to develop one's own personality. My parents raised me this way out of misconstrued perceptions of love and duty! They tried to break my spirit! They almost succeeded! I always felt guilty if I did not adapt to what was required of my family, or of any group in which I live or work. But I finally am freeing myself with the realization that it is the church that is guilty and its teachings that are guilty, not me!

∞

REPRESSION OF FEMININITY

Look at the chastening of Eve in Genesis, the sinful one, the one who was created with the inherent character flaw. Sexual repression of women began early in the Judeo/Christian tradition, developed by patriarchs, most likely in their desire to stamp out the traditional Goddess religion which gave respect and power to women. Sometimes a belief in the female deity produced a matrilineal religion which passed name and property through the female line. But patriarchs wanted to assure their own positions. A patriarchal religion gradually developed in which all women have been considered by religious society to be sinful by definition. This seems extreme, when stated baldly, but the indoctrination methods and results have been subtle and pervasive in the development of our social mores. Think of the woman who does not value her body, who sees it as something that belongs to others automatically: her parents, husband, and children. Think of the woman who sees her body as the total of who she is; her physical beauty as her sole value, *herself*.

Throughout the centuries, we have learned to adore men, serve them in various ways, physically, sexually, emotionally; thus they have developed an automatic sense of power. The very assumption by men of their superiority is a subtle form of female abuse. The Christian church has been the backbone of western civilization throughout most of the last 2000 years. One cannot study the history of western society for the last two millennia without an intensive study of Christian development and influence on social and historical happenings.

Christianity has dispensed the idea of male superiority liberally. Men in church positions taught, and often still teach, that concerns of the body are wrong, and that feminine physical beauty is sinful, because it is an attraction. Carried to an extreme, this position creates mentally ill men who want to punish, eliminate, and kill women whom they see as sinful objects, often simply because they are women. Remember the burnings of witches during the Middle Ages in Europe. Witness the mass killing of the women engineering students at École Polytechnique in Montreal on December 6, 1989. From the position that women's bodies are inherently wrong because of their ability to attract men, we women have developed a loss of regard for our own bodies. Men have often used us, blaming us for their own needs to abuse others. We have developed the feeling that our bodies have no right to be free, the feeling that our bodies have no rights. This is a reaction still prevalent in Christian and Muslim societies today. As a girl growing up in the atmosphere of the Christian church, I developed an inability to be myself, a feeling of unnaturalness about my body, and about myself as a whole. I often felt, particularly in church atmospheres, that I could not breathe. I became extremely self-conscious. What was the accepted norm for behaviour? For even moving, walking? Was I perfect enough? I allowed myself no errors. Therefore no movement. I confined my feelings, my movements. I became stiff, literally. I held myself tight. I rejected the essential feminine me. **My inside suicide.**

∞

SEPARATION FROM THE SELF

I was separating from myself. I lost my identity in the church environment. My personality was taken away from me. I learned to identify with a sense of responsibility to others only, a virtue which church societies extol for women. Spontaneity and *joie de vivre* are repressed under this attitude, for responsibility usually means denying the self in response to taking care of the needs of others: a loss of personality. After years of Jungian therapy and much reading and reflection, I realize that righteous judgment made me, as a young girl, and young woman, feel just the same as a rape victim feels: disempowered, helpless, dirty, shamed, guilty, and inadequate. My fault.

It was very clear to me that my Christian duty was to my church and to my family. I experienced a sense of *examination* from within the church community, an incredible violation of my being! I have friends and acquaintances that have also experienced these terrible feelings of persecution, which turn into a persecution of the self. The self becomes numb. As a high school teacher, I have sometimes over the years seen girls inflict pain on themselves, actually cutting their arms and legs with knives, in order to 'feel' something! Others became anorexic or bulimic, forcing themselves to purge their food after eating. They were denying themselves their basic need to self-nourish. I see these actions as a form of self-punishment, self-judgment for not being good enough to attain the perfection set up by judgmental families and churches. The physical body, and what we do to it, is a direct reflection of what is happening in our minds. Mind, body, and spirit are interconnected.

∞

THE INSIDIOUS NATURE OF CONTROL

There is an insidious circular result in churches' control of members. If one has been controlled by others, one feels a need to control others in return. I certainly felt this. That may be one reason I went into teaching. The altruistic feeling of helping others in a profession such as teaching is strong. But the sense of influence over young lives gave me a feeling of power, of strength, as I assisted learning. It was a real ego trip! I loved it! I am sure that many teachers go into the profession in order to exert control. Unfortunately, some use their positions of authority in a ruthless manner. In the classroom, I felt that my opinions were validated. I loved my profession, and was generally very effective, but not as effective in my schools as I could have been without feelings of fear coming from my restricted background.

Yet I have felt it my duty to give advice to friends who have problems. I know now that when we give advice we want to 'own' someone else's journey; we rob them of control of themselves. We patronize them, which involves less respect. We create a judgmental attitude. To counter the judgmental attitude of church teachings, a girl needs a wise mother who is able to look at church teachings with perspective, who is able to teach her daughter to use intuition and common sense as she learns to interpret for herself, to think freely. People work, live, and love better if they are self-activated. I am still learning not to give advice to friends and family. If I speak in 'I' statements, explain that an experience happened to *me*, then my words are accepted and heard much better. My friends do not then feel that I am judging them, trying to control their lives. Each is on her own journey.

My mother was so caught up in her own spirituality, so bound by religious conformity and consequent sense of duty to husband, family and church, that she was able to give me little guidance in using common sense, which I needed to develop confidence. In the atmosphere of control from within and from without, I felt my environment closing in around me; I have been fearful of the outside world with which I was not familiar. Fearful of others judging me. I have as a result, actually developed environmental illness. My world has closed in physically, as my body has listened to the messages conveyed by my conscious and subconscious mind.

∞

THE RESULTS OF CONFORMITY

There is a basic tribal need for conformity in society. Insistence on uniformity is the way a culture weeds out radical elements in order to survive, to strengthen itself. This can be carried to extremes in social attempts to force compliance from members. The church has used and abused this need for conformity over the last 2000 years, although conformity was initially needed to survive and thrive as an institution. Conformity evolved into control. Then Church implied the perfection of men simply by birthright, bringing feelings of shame on women who have been imbued with the need to care for men, whom we have regarded as our betters, and often our masters. We feel good, and worthy, if we bow to their cause. Even enlightened, educated, and informed women find it difficult to break from ingrained patterns. Many realize what has happened, and decide not to break from tradition. The problems with family and friends would be too great. Most importantly, breaking with tradition involves a total remaking of oneself, a rediscovery of oneself, and a consequent remaking of one's person: a horrendous task emotionally, possibly involving financial and social changes in one's life, which indeed seems to be a daunting undertaking. Usually when women finally awaken, we do so with an incredible sense of anger at our loss. I was taught to feel responsibility to the community around me, of the importance of fitting in, of being the good woman. I was expected to take up the slack when my mother became ill; I was expected to help manage the household; I provided feminine emotional support for my fracturing family. As a teenager I railed against the responsibility, demanding the return to normality in my childhood home, while at the same time glorying in the respect of my additional roles. I now realize how I was programmed and used. My anger has been intense; my sadness is continual. Pushing beyond this requires an ongoing supreme effort.

Social expectations of young women often cause an intolerance of others with different views. Being told that her spiritual society is better than any other religious aspect of society, a young woman such as I was can feel crippled, yet not understand what the problems are, thinking instead of herself as the problem, as the one who can't fit into the mold. I became very depressed; so have millions of others like me.

THE INSIDE SUICIDE: SHATTERING ILLUSIONS

    To be a good member of a churchgoing family, one must fit into the mold. To differ is to bring dishonour to one's family, and to oneself. We have been taught to love, honour, and obey, whether or not we swore those vows in marriage. I felt smothered by the dilemma of my religion. I wanted to be loyal to a church which had fostered me, but at the same time I felt that my spirituality was being repressed. I consider this to be an insidious and very real form of sexual bias. I was denied, as many, many other women have been, the most fundamental of freedoms, that of the ability to seek and fulfill my own identity!

∞

ROLE REVERSAL

Some women felt that they could not be themselves as women. Some, like George Eliot, Willa Cather, have written with the persona of a man. Some, like George Sands, have even dressed as a man, for the outward sign of a woman is her dress. One friend told me of a costume party she and her husband hosted, in which the women came dressed as men, and the men as women. Great fun! But what my friend experienced the most during this was a complete feeling of power and freedom dressed as a man, with the ability within the situation to assume the role of strength and dominance.

Women like me feel dishonest, like traitors, if we question church teachings and traditions. We feel shame for not fitting into the mold, of not doing the expected womanly thing. We feel we cannot speak out against our families, our churches, against the traditions which have fostered us. We question what right we as women actually have to voice opinions on church practices, which have served society well for over 2000 years. What right do we have to have opinions on spiritual matters? We are not trained in theology. We feel we must leave these matters to the clergy. We feel deep guilt, intense shame, for even thinking of defying the overpowering authority of the Church. But to fulfill ourselves as people we need to accept that we must speak our minds freely. To everyone, including our husbands. Some of my friends do not tell their husbands what they truly believe in their own hearts about church tenets and practices. But if we adjust our actions for the sake of our husbands, we are not honest with ourselves, we are not free as individuals. We must overcome the fear of being judged by others, the fear of needing their approval. Even with a supportive husband, overcoming the judgment of others has been, and still is, an incredibly difficult task for me!

∞

ATMOSPHERE

Church experiences are alluring simply because of the physical beauty of the setting. The physical grandeur of cathedrals, the quiet peace of wooden pews and stained glass windows, the simple cross at the front, the elegant altar draperies, are all meant to conspire to the feeling of being surrounded by peace and protection. The music, often organ music, emphasizes the atmosphere of grandeur, and inspires feelings of loving protection, also implied in hymns: "God sees the little sparrow fall". A person can meditate, and feel safe, and right in such an impressive atmosphere. People adore better if they are worshiping in awe-inspiring places, purposely built to impress, and in fact to subjugate one's insecurities, one's questions about God and life and relationships. People adore better if they are awed by the formality of ritual. Church rituals are meant to convey tradition through continuity of symbolism, repetition, and order.

Many people today, perceiving the world as chaotic, and meaningless, filled with evil, seek explanations from the church. Ritual conveys comfort for people who fear change and loss. But ritual simultaneously conveys a heaviness, a grayness, somberness, which affects the depths of the being, transmuting feelings which last forever. People take into their hearts the feeling of the church as the one right, moral institution, unchangeable, immutable in its strength, lacking in true compassion in its impersonality. For centuries church institutions have explored and debated the meanings of God, the qualities of religious experience. Bertrand Russell has said, "To live like this means to give up hope of an answer. We respect what is mysterious, while all the while, we seek to unravel it." Living like this restricts our enjoyment of life. It fills us with hesitation, with self-doubt about our own worthiness to experience life to the fullest. I almost always left a church service with a feeling of depression, sometimes oppression. I didn't identify it as such at the time, but as I bring the feelings back to the surface now, I realize the depression I had absorbed. There was a falseness to the experience. As a child, I couldn't have stated what it was. I just felt lucky to be in such a community, but depressed.

SUPPORT

The church, renowned for wonderful deeds of support in communities, has shone over the centuries, with generation after generation helping those who need strength. Caring by the church has taken two forms: support for those who are within the church community, and support for those who are outside it. Both forms can be positive, as well as negative. As I write this, the devastating earthquake in Haiti is very much in the news. Governments and aid organizations from around the world are pouring assistance into this already damaged and impoverished nation. Haiti's own government seems to have become almost ineffectual under the enormity of the tragedy. The huge amount of aid being sent from those of us who are so much more fortunate is laudable, and necessary. It will certainly be well-appreciated. Yet, amid the numerous daily commentaries on the tragedy in the media, one commentator said that we have to be careful how far we help a nation in such trouble, for if we assist to the point of control, then the nation never really finds its own way, never really learns to assist itself, as it climbs back to a semblance of normality. The same is true of our involvement in Afghanistan. How much can we help before we damage? There are many who say we damage simply by trying to help anyone there at all. Then there are those who want the western alliance to have as much influence as possible in controlling and creating friendly governments in countries such as Afghanistan. Motives and results can scramble relationships.

Tolerance for the spiritual and physical conditions of others *can* be very discriminative in reality. People intend to be the rescuers, but easily become persecutors, especially if the rescue is given for reasons of *duty*. Witness the wonderfully perceptive novel of Barbara Kingsolver, *The Poisonwood Bible*, which illustrates the destructive force of missionary work in Africa on both the native people, and the story's missionary family. Considering my own belief system, whether religious or political, as better than someone else's is always destructive. In helping to restore Haiti, for example, we must be very careful not to impose our value systems on Haitians' way of life. There must come a point at which we continue to provide aid only if requested. Giving aid rarely works unless the people helped have asked for assistance. Feelings of responsibility for others can become very negative if we become judgmental of those we are assisting. If we begin to feel superior, we often feel bitter, as though someone is taking advantage of us. We become drained, burned out, a signal that something is wrong with our attitudes. We feel false. When I give, I give of *myself, of my own spirit!* I recognize that caring for others, in fortune and in misfortune, can bring communities together wonderfully. The measure of a civilization has always been its ability to care for its weakest members, but I feel that this works only *as long as these members are able to voice their wish for the help.* I still often wonder if the ability to consider all people as equal is possible. People automatically compare. Comparisons are odious.

People join church communities to find support and compassion. They often find true compassion and strength from others there. But the compassion they find is from a community which loves them *because* of their troubles, *because* they need support. It is a community which loves them because they have joined. This is ambiguous for many church attendees, who on the one hand feel protection from the church, and on the other, feel duty to show compassion to those in trouble, and guilt if they don't. This system sets up a very judgmental atmosphere, for who can decide who needs help? Who needs to be invasively encouraged, or prayed for? Churchgoers can become very secretive, as a result, portraying only strength, in an effort to ward off the pity of others. But it has been my experience that one of the worst problems in relationships has been the keeping of secrets, those hidden truths in our hearts which affect our psyches from the bottom up, those secrets which boil up with emotion the longer they are repressed, boil up and erupt in emotional and physical illness. Secrets poison.

∞

RESPECT

Many people go to church, saying to themselves, "Am I not good for being here?" I have heard friends boast about going to different churches every Sunday of their holidays away from home. My Dad used to do the same. On holiday we had to find the closest United Church every Sunday. Weren't we good for being there! A system of who can be the most pious, who can show the most compassion. A competitive atmosphere! It is usually the women who take in others under their wings, help others. Women who do the most for others within a church community are respected the most, both by men and by women. Respect is what we all aim for! But how hard to admit our weaknesses when we are the ones who have to show continual strength! Therefore, guilt arises if we talk about illness, daily problems and struggles. We are admired as women if we show no weakness, only strength, the ability to give to others. We are admired if we live through adverse situations without complaint, without railing against the vagaries of life which have affected us adversely. How contrary to human nature to repress our feelings so! Very unhealthy! Vicious circles!

Women brought up as I was feel dishonest if we question church teachings and traditions. We feel traitors to our tribal group, to our society. We feel shame if we don't fit into the mold, if we do the unexpected, even if we unconsciously try to find our own voices. We feel we cannot speak out against the church, for what right do we as women have to have opinions on the church, opinions on spiritual matters? We feel shame even thinking of questioning the overpowering authority of the church.

Many church denominations across the world have spent years and years, and millions and millions building grand cathedrals to the 'Glory of God': an effort to command respect. These institutions have often broken their people physically and financially in their demands on their flocks. Many have rebelled, as have the people of Quebec in the past half century. People become disillusioned and bitter when controlled to such an extent.

∞

OWNERSHIP

In many cultures, including the Judeo-Christian and Muslim cultures, men have traditionally felt, and still feel, that *they* own women. Even today in many enlightened elements of these traditions, men still see women as objects they can buy, sell, and treat as they wish, even put to death with impunity: beliefs sanctioned by their religious communities. One of my friends has told me the following story, which precipitated her marriage breakup. After the birth of her second child, she was having difficulty getting the baby to sleep at night. She was exhausted from trying to take care of an active toddler, who demanded attention all day, and staying up all night with a baby, who stayed awake all night. One evening about midnight, she decided to walk around the block with the baby in his carriage, because the movement soothed him, sometimes lulling him to sleep. One of the young men boarders in her house saw her leaving the house so late for a walk, and asked to accompany her, feeling it too dangerous for her to be out alone in North Toronto at that time of night. As they returned to the house, her husband appeared, flying into a rage at seeing his wife in the company of another man. He berated her harshly, then dragged her up the stairs and raped her, to teach her not to besmirch his honour again. He felt that he owned his wife, that she was his. The marriage broke. I admire her strength and courage.

While treating their women with disdain on the one hand, men have often, ironically, treated women as objects to be worshiped. They idealized them for the roles they play in society in supporting men's activities, both physically and emotionally. Many men revere their women for their piety, their spiritual connections. The Renaissance literary tradition of the Romance of the Rose, in which women were idealized as perfect, flawless beings, put women on pedestals from which many people today hundreds of years later, still have not allowed us to descend. But no person is perfect. Everyone has flaws. To live up to the perfection which men demand of women is a huge burden, taking away a woman's ability to live life on her own terms. Women accede in this in order to gain respect and love. It is almost as though some families feel that the more they adore their women, 'respect' them, the more they can ask of them, use them, putting them down in various ways. Many women I know, who remain on their pedestals, love to boast about how much they are adored by their men.

∞

ROLES

In dysfunctional families, the family subconsciously assigns a role for each member to play, to be responsible for, and to live out. The family does this to protect its own survival. This usually happens in alcoholic families, for example. But this sets up problems of anger, rebellion, and depression among the various members. Families work best if roles are interchangeable. Each person in a family needs to be encouraged to explore his or her own abilities on his or her own terms. Family duties and functions are best carried out if they are interchanged from one member to another. To be expected to be the main caregiver, the one who supplies the emotional support and strength for the family for a lifetime is a tremendous burden. Similarly, to be expected to be the one who supports the family financially in a difficult business environment is an equally heavy burden.

Expectations of feminine perfection have led to the demand for women to be loyal to men. Men often devise ways to keep women pleasing them in order to assure their loyalty. My father adored me because I took care of my sick mother and our family. I lived for his love and approval; it kept me going. But I was not developing myself according to my own rights, my own needs. My father needed me to keep his job and our household running as smoothly and effectively as possible.

∞

APPROVAL

Many men resent any time which their wives and daughters spend with others. They want their total attention for themselves. I have friends and acquaintances whose husbands have become terribly jealous if their wives spent any time with friends or connections outside the home. How incredibly demeaning! I have friends whose husbands have resented their wives' friendships with me, fearing that I am a corrupting influence on them and their traditional family structure. They have wanted to control and approve of the connections their wives made. Some of my women friends have felt that their first duty was to their husband's needs, and that if he was uncomfortable with his wife having me as a friend, then they should limit their connections with me. This has hurt me deeply. For the sake of peace in the family, many women still seek the approval of husbands first, before all. To be totally functional, a woman needs autonomy in her decisions about her life. She does not ignore her family. She makes decisions based on family considerations.

∞

INDEPENDENCE

I remember one male co-worker, a history teacher, suddenly asking me one day who was the 'boss' in my relationship with my husband. The teacher had had a marriage breakup himself, and was having a rough time with his new relationship. He was trying to understand relationships he saw as functioning well. I was flattered. I remember telling him that sometimes my husband made the decisions, and sometimes I did, for I might make the decision at one time about an area on which he had decided last time. We usually discussed decisions together before deciding. And I realized that my marriage is relatively good compared to many, and that the methods my husband and I use work for us. Independence in thought and action, the emotional and financial ability to run one's own life, seem to be the key.

∞

PROGRAMMED SCHIZOPHRENIA

The results of this tradition of honouring men are often psychologically complicated. A woman who feels that her differing views are 'disloyal' will feel guilt. She may try to mold herself into thinking as her husband does, as her husband wishes. She will gradually learn to think of herself as secondary, certainly inferior, feeling that the woman's main purpose in life is to act as a support for her husband. Women are the sex supplied with compassion and the ability to connect through emotion. These attitudes of inequality fuel feelings of insecurity for both sexes. Men and women naturally delight in life, delight in others, and find strength. But if patriarchal systems of society teach repression of enjoyment, people like me feel very much at odds with ourselves, literally 'out of place'.

One of my friends told me that when she went to church, she felt as if her personal power was totally taken away. From the experience of becoming very ill, she knew that she couldn't allow loss of her own power again, so she stopped attending church, where she felt powerless. I can remember, as a teenager particularly, often feeling terribly awkward as I tried to please people in our congregation. This influenced my view of myself in my own peer group, as well. I thought my awkwardness, my feeling of not fitting in, was my fault. I felt much less than the perfect ideal of a teenage daughter in my religious society, or indeed in any part of my society. This schizophrenic feeling of thinking that I could never be who I was 'supposed' to be, created havoc in my heart and mind, often bringing anger against others. I gradually became withdrawn on the one hand, yet bitter and outspoken on the other. Like my friend who became so ill, I also lost my power. Churches are too dictatorial, whether they think they are or not, trying to control the actions and thoughts of young people with the intention of molding them into the spiritual life of goodness and therefore safety They are not serving people well. Institutions and parents who try to protect their children from the realities of life do not really protect children in the long run, but instead do harm by repressing their abilities to grow and to survive in society on their own terms. Children need the freedom of discovery and experience, with the protection of a trusted adult at home who gives guidance and advice.

THE INSIDE SUICIDE: SHATTERING ILLUSIONS

    Religious institutions have failed people like me by not teaching us to follow our own intuition, to develop our own common sense in life, to form a realization of our own abilities. These qualities are usually instilled by understanding parents, who lead through example, and who are available to give advice when needed. When a religious institution assumes the role of a parent, it restricts feelings and thoughts enormously. I felt such a sense of shock and anger when I first realized the extent of the damage which the perfidy of the church has had on my own soul! My parents believed totally in the efficacy of a Christian life, the goodness of a spiritual life. I have friends who seem on the surface to have survived such a life well enough themselves, but whose children have not, exhibiting antisocial behaviour. Sometimes a young person will take a job as far away as possible from the parents' home, in order to distance themselves from parental control, and family problems. The harm caused by indoctrination is carried on from generation to generation.

∞

POWER BY PROTECTION

Women have to guard against protection becoming exploitation. If a woman is exploited, her feeling of ownership of her own person is taken away. Traditionally, men have protected our safety, and therefore our honour; through this, they achieve their own purpose of protecting themselves emotionally from the hurt of losing a daughter, or losing family honour.

A woman's sexual reputation has been connected to her family's sense of honour since ancient Jewish tradition. In many cultures, a woman whose sexual reputation has been compromised by sex outside of marriage, or even rape which is not her fault, is shunned as unclean. Most of Western society has become liberated now in attitudes to sex. But stigma is still often attached to a woman who is viewed as "damaged or used goods." Traditionally, women have been expected to keep themselves sexually innocent until marriage. We are charged with the responsibility of the social code, even though we are often unable to defend ourselves against assault. Men have adopted the idea that they need to 'protect' women by seeing to their sexual purity. This idea of protection has been extended to include protecting the woman from many aspects of life, usually the aspects which include enjoyment and challenge, realms which men have reserved for themselves.

Women thrive if they are treated equally in relationships in our society, not protected. Under protection, they acquire a sense of inferiority. The relationship with the 'protector' becomes skewed, not one of respect for each other. The protected one feels indebted to the protector, and therefore often resentful.

When I found the man I married, I had conflicting feelings about expecting my husband to protect me, to keep me safe in many situations. He usually refused to do so. I continued to maintain my own independence, making my own decisions. I'm so thankful that our relationship evolved this way. I realize now that I would not have adapted as a compliant wife. How unhappy I would have been! And with what results for my marriage!

SEXUAL PURITY

Sexual purity is highly symbolic of honour. To many men, a woman's sexual purity is symbolic of her purity in all aspects of her life. It symbolizes her ability to provide love, affection, emotional and physical comfort for her husband, her family, her society. In many parts of the world today, and even in many parts of our 'enlightened' western society, a woman is considered of no value if she is not pure sexually. It is she who is bound to keep herself sexually pure before marriage, whether she loses her virginity of her own free will or not. Systematic rape of women has been one way a conquering army has controlled and subjugated a conquered people. The idea that a woman has to be pure, intact, in order to be wholesome and a good wife, devalues her worth as an individual. This concept can destroy a whole society, demoralize it, at the least, if its women have been raped.

Often parental love of a daughter is given conditionally, as my parents' was, depending on my maintaining my sexual virginity, and by extension, my spiritual purity. I knew that I would be considered very selfish by my family if I challenged our traditional mores. This is the primary way society has controlled women, forcing us to lose our sense of independence. Sexual caution is indeed desirable with the dangers, both emotional and physical, in today's society. Young girls like me, however, identifying with mothers who see their primary role as secondary to their husbands, who see their duty to indoctrinate their daughters with the same mores in order to raise them as appropriately acceptable young women, do damage to their daughters. Young girls need the love and approval of their fathers. If they strive to please to too great an extent, aiming for the perfection which religions set up as a goal, they lose themselves as they grow into womanhood. Society has not served us well by forcing a sense of protection on us. The consequent burden on women is onerous.

Over the last 2000 years, since the beginning of Christianity, the developing church assumed the role of protector of its flock, especially of its women. This role was not inherent in early Christian traditions, but gradually evolved as a need to protect members from persecution. But the role became abused as church leaders realized the potential power in being a protector. Thus its role as an overly protective parent has gradually assured its place in society, for it has implied guilt and consequent sin if its prescriptions were not obeyed. Telling people they are bad, evil, is an effective way of maintaining control. It is also demeaning, and harmful to life in its destruction of free thinking and freedom of action. All done in the name of 'protection'. There are all kinds of benefits for the clergy and the religious institutions which control by fear: benefits of power and respect are the main ones. The more power one has, the more one's position is assured.

∞

IDEALISM

When men regarded women as needing protection, men started to worship women as perfect. Literary tradition in Western Europe is rife with this throughout the centuries. During the Renaissance, duels were fought in the name of women. The recent war in Afghanistan in our own era has been justified to a good extent as a war to free Afghani women. A reverse form of protection! The irony of it! As far back as Ancient Greece, tales of women like Helen of Troy inspired men to heroic deeds. So romantic in fiction! So terribly hard to live with if you are a woman actually trying to live up to the ideals of perfection! Women have been loved, not for who they are, but for the *ideal* of who they are in the male mind. Women in our present-day society are still encouraged by every aspect of the media to be beautiful, feminine, modest, and often pure in sex. And men boast about their conquests. Many women in Western society have found that they must *look* sexually attractive, but not actually *be* sexually attractive. As a young woman, I did not feel right about having fun by being sexually attractive.

Paradoxically, in return for physical protection from the harshness of life, women have felt that men should be taken care of, catered to, waited on. 'Perfect' women have learned to conform to the expectation of being dutiful selfless caregivers. I did this for my Dad when my mother became ill and died. A woman must continually give of her 'anima', her female spirit, for a woman is admired by a man if she *appears* to be selfless to her family. I have women friends who give selflessly of themselves to their communities in order to gain the respect and admiration of their husbands. Communities love and extol their volunteers who give time and effort to the care and betterment of those needing help. These are worthwhile goals of any community, for the strength of a society can be gauged by the care it takes of its weaker members. The problem for me occurs when people are encouraged to do care giving to the exclusion of taking care of their own needs, and when such people are extolled, put on pedestals as being better than others. Power becomes skewed if we think of ourselves as better than those we help, better than those under our protection.

Women can feel intense guilt and shame if they feel that they are not being 'womanly', upholding the image of being the expected selfless, effacing caregivers. I admire greatly others who are able to give of themselves to community betterment; I myself cannot do much without feeling that something is wrong for me. I feel as though I am patronizing the people to whom I am giving assistance. Yet the training of my background is strong: I feel guilt that I cannot give of myself in community aid. I can no longer be the selfless caregiver I had to be so early in my childhood and teenage years when my mother was dying. The guilt of my lack of ability to give extensive community support at this point in my life is keen. If I step into a care giving role, I become divided within myself. I feel that it is my duty to perform the care-giving role demanded of me, but at the same time I feel used and abused, and so deplore my inability to stand up for my own independence. I felt when I was called upon to perform this role, that there was something the matter with me if I was not happy taking care of my family. Women require self-discovery and self-fulfillment as much as men do. Anybody does. Honest self-fulfillment through service to others requires a rare self-knowledge and self-awareness. Otherwise, service to others is soul-destroying. We are exploited by society's expectation of women's duty to their families, at the expense of our own independent development.

Power by protection becomes so twisted in our relationships! I think that it is impossible for equal relationships to exist if protection is involved.

∞

COMPLICITY ON THE PART OF WOMEN

In spite of the problems of care giving for women, there has been a skillful complicity on the part of women in their adaptation to the male vision of women's place in society. Many of us feel useless unless we are respected by our society. This becomes a form of control by those who strive to make women feel guilty if they do not succumb to the traditional care-giving role. Many women in western society look to the masculine, patriarchal church as a father-figure, needing to continue their childhood feelings of finding support and approval from their fathers. As a result, an unwritten code of behaviour has developed among women brought up in church societies, in which the tacit rule of the group is that women may belong *as long as they act according to expectations of the group!* Even today when I walk into women's groups, especially church groups, I feel an intense need to comply to the unwritten code of behaviour in order to be accepted. It is hard to deviate from this, to break from expected tradition. Heilbrun expresses the secondary position thusly: "In the last years of the twentieth century, it is unclear whether women who refer to themselves as, for example, Mrs. Thomas Smith know what servitude they are representing in that nomenclature. The same might be said today of women who exchange their last name for their husband's." (p.85)

Throughout history, women have had to agree to this collusion often from fear for their lives. Conform or die, or at the very least, be outcast, has been the practice toward women for thousands of years, and still is today in many parts of the world. How many women were burned at the stake or hung as witches because they dared to think for themselves? But some of us who collude, the majority of us in most parts of our history, suffer feelings of hypocrisy, feelings of being used by our society.

I have watched women who finally achieve positions of power, having gained responsibility over others, become very cruel to other women now under their control. Women managers in business can take out their bitterness on others so easily, if their own early lives have been ones of repression and lack of recognition. I wonder how many women managers actually get the respect they deserve as people who have earned their positions? How many actually respect themselves enough to find contentment in their work? How many realize that they actually have attained these positions because of their own creative abilities to invent? Many feel they must continue to fight for their power, or lose it. "I went through it, suffered under repression of women, and rose to a position of power; therefore these women under me must do the same" is often their attitude. It is the lack of recognition of a woman's worth, the subtle repression of her because she is a female, which is the hardest for women to recognize. I watched as one of my school principals, a woman, rose to a position of power as a leader within the county system. I watched her hold her own in the male world of administrative positions, yet at the same time, try to maintain her feminine intuition. She did her best to be aware of the men in the school who were putting down women staff members, and to call them on it. She understood, to a good extent, that it's a matter of being allowed to be yourself. She helped the women staff members, including me, who had problems one way or another. Those who considered men to be the ultimate authoritarian figures did not appreciate her attempts. I didn't, until later, when I gained more perspective on the situation. It took me distance and awareness to gain this appreciation.

∞

EXPECTATIONS

What woman, brought up in a loving middle-class home thinks of herself as repressed? Nevertheless, here most of us are, still struggling with our views of ourselves as we try to find our way. To be a good wife, a good mother, and a good business woman seems to be too much to achieve at times, polarities demanding perfection. As women in a modern world, how do we reconcile ourselves to such differing and complex expectations which we have set up for ourselves? Churches which take seriously the role of women in society today, need to 'mother' their women so that women can better understand their own strengths and the strengths of others. I think that if we have strong mother images, strong mother symbolism in our social institutions, then we can more easily let go of trying to control others. Control of others, even though helping them, results in a feeling of indebtedness, and is extremely destructive.

∞

CARING

Genuine caring can lead to genuine connection with others. Mutual support is encouraged by churches, as people have strong social needs to belong, to be accepted and loved as members of a community. If only a *seeming* tolerance of others who are different is extended, however, a sense of superiority in the tolerance, then an inequality among members evolves, causing the ones aided to feel inferior, and therefore repressed. If caring means *fixing* then equality is skewed, and harm takes place.

There can be a great comfort in belonging to a community such as a church, but it can so easily lead to feelings of repression. Communities necessarily have codes of behaviour, unwritten ones, as well as written ones. I find that I have to be constantly aware of what is happening within myself when I am with a church group, or with any formed group. Constantly vigilant. Repression of feelings, holding in, leads to depression in our souls. How can I find comfort in an institution, which although it fostered me, causes me to be so hyper-vigilant in order to protect myself from its invasive need to control me with its own limited set of rules? I realize that the church is trying to protect me, but I am in an agonizing dilemma, needing to belong, and yet needing my independence! My independence of thought and action has to win out! I cannot compromise on this. My centre must hold, or I am nothing!

∞

SPIRITUAL DEVELOPMENT

Churches and religious institutions provide settings for spiritual renewal and development. As a young adult I could occasionally find quiet in my mind, resuscitation of my soul in the Christian church setting. The rhythm of services, the rhythm of the words, the hypnotic connection to others in the music: these parts of the drama all contribute to the warmth of the atmosphere. Church ritual is a genuine art form which is very beautiful. Religious rites enhance the depth of spiritual experience, working on the *heart* level to help us connect to our own higher selves, and thus find the Divine within ourselves. The controller's language is often hypnotically beautiful!

∞

SACRED BEAUTY

But Christianity is such a small way of knowing the sacred. It can initiate a spirituality, but it is too narrow a viewpoint for understanding what is truly sacred. Sacredness is a blue heron on the end of a dock in the early morning. It is looking into someone's eyes and seeing beauty. Sacredness is the sound of waves breaking on the beach as you wake in the morning. Spiders on the cottage wall. The warmth of sand underfoot on a beach. The swish of wind in trees on a humid day. Raccoon kits climbing down the hollow tree on their maiden voyage. Sacredness is acceptance of my journey in my friend's eyes, her 'Good for you!' response. These things are love. Each, a holiness.

The *heart* creates love amongst peoples, the *mind* fragmentation and compartmentalization. The Church has been an intellectual institution over its history, debating dogma endlessly. People within the Church have often divided the same branch of religion into various sects with slightly differing beliefs. Dogma separates peoples from their spiritual depths. Miracles have been considered acts of faith, having nothing to do with the body's ability to heal itself. Miracles necessarily stem from a person's own belief in the ability to heal oneself. Disease is not sent to test one's faith. *Disease is a reaction to one's faith*, to one's belief system of life. The propensity for the disease may be there in our genes to begin with, but the disease erupts if one is consciously or subconsciously in conflict. Physical reaction is a reaction to the mental state of mind, as healers like Louise Hay, Carolyn Myss, and Sheila Pennington have shown.

balance: the body, mind, and spirit connection

True faith involves a fusion of one's own body, mind, and spirit; a union which can come about only with an understanding of oneself from one's heart. Accepting and living with one's body, accepting responsibility for one's life, for one's capabilities is paramount. There is such a fine balance between pushing too hard, and the fear of overwhelming responsibility, in reaction to excessive demands. Excessive fear creates an **Inside suicide.**

THE INSIDE SUICIDE: SHATTERING ILLUSIONS

    I am finally awakening! True faith is respect for my body and mind and spirit to such a deep extent that they are united into my soul, and thus with the Divine. If I am ill-at-ease with myself, I need to examine the parts of my life which are out of balance, often a very difficult task in the hectic lifestyles many of us live today. If we make time to regain balance will we regain our centres.

∞

CREATING SACRED SPACE

A passage from Sherry Ruth Anderson and Patricia Hopkins relates their interview with Twylah Nitsch, who as a child received parental support for finding her own spirituality:

"I was taught that our space is sacred and we are responsible for what happens in it,' she told us. 'We have a place that we are born into, and parents who taught us the principles we use in carrying out our mission in life. I learned from my grandfather that I had a place where I tied my rope, and no matter who pulled on it, or tried to separate me from it, I could always go back to my center. Everyone has a rope, but most people's ropes are dangling because they have no place to tie them."

"Does that mean that your rope is tied to something inside you?" we asked.
"Yes," Twylah replied, "but in my tradition it's also tied to the place where you were born."
"So," we persisted, "how does that work if you travel a lot or have to move away from your birthplace?"
"It means that you take your sacred space with you," Twylah answered."If that feeling of security has been developed from the beginning and built up over a period of years, you can take it with you anywhere you go. Each of us carries our sacred space within us, and our challenge is to live from it throughout our life's journey, throughout our earth walk."
Anderson and Hopkins, (p. 38.)

My own journey has been, and still is difficult, at times agonizing, I think because my own spiritual centre was repressed. It was very hard for me to feel a sense of confidence in my own abilities to find my place in life. I have had to face the depth and power of my own anger as I have realized the damage done to me and other women by society's 'good' intentions. Usually, as we change in life, we go through periods of intense anger and criticism of the institutions and forces which we are in the process of rejecting, as we transform ourselves into newness. It has been hard to realize and accept this anger in myself as a necessary and good force in my change. The pendulum of emotional feelings has swung widely as I go through periods of intensive self-searching, as I return to a sense of centeredness.

I lost my way, as one usually does doing this kind of work. There is no map, or final destination. I lost my need to fulfill certain obligations to my family or society in order to take my respected place in the community. This feeling of being utterly lost is a necessary stage on this journey, if I was to truly change. For most women, it is a feeling of going into the wilderness, a feeling of utter darkness in the soul. Anderson and Hopkins describe the difficulty of facing the journey, which they call 'leaving home':

> Leaving home can take us right up to the edge of the unknown. But if the timing is not right, or if we are not yet brave enough, we may choose to postpone, or avoid going through it. Because the uncertainty and aloneness that result can be intensely uncomfortable, the wish to escape can be almost overwhelming. Anything that distracts us from looking beneath the surface of our lives will tempt us: a new relationship, a different job, moving to a different city, or going to the country, taking up the latest form of exercise, attending one more workshop or seminar. However, the danger of not leaving home is that we can spend the rest of our lives hiding from ourselves. Anderson and Tomkins, (p. 64)

Even after years of therapy and personal work, I still have regressions in my feelings and thinking patterns, finding myself repressing my thoughts and abilities, thinking negative thoughts about myself, losing my confidence. I realize that I am constantly growing, constantly discovering myself, and not always at an even speed. Depending on what else is going on in my life, I still sometimes slow down, or even stand still in my sense of self-awareness, in my sense of developing who I am. I am still learning, late and slowly, how to carry my sacred space with me. I am still learning to have confidence that my sacred space is really here, inside me, with me all the time, a force I can return to if I have temporarily lost it. It is now fairly solid in me, rarely shaken.

RESULTS OF MY INSIDE SUICIDE

My body has shown me clearly the lack of ease I have had with myself. In mid-life, I developed allergies fairly severely, becoming sensitive to so much in our environment: perfumes, cleaning chemicals, car emissions, as well as allergies to the natural beauty around me of trees, flowers, grass, the earth itself. I am learning to heal my body's extreme reactions to the very acts of living. I have been closing out life itself, withdrawing within. Yet again, just two years ago, I developed rheumatoid arthritis, signaling my body's inability to move forward in life. I have been fearing my own voice, my own power. I am trying to let myself go, to enjoy what is here for me now! I am writing this, expressing myself with relative freedom. Do I still feel censure? Yes! But I am trying to free myself of its power. I am trying to unite the needs of my body, mind, and spirit into my own spiritual sensibility.

In a desire to strive for true spirituality, people can easily fall into the trap of trying to be totally sincere, totally loving, uncritical, especially in church settings. I certainly became afraid of offending anyone. This attitude hampered me in my career; I was afraid of voicing my opinion. Trying to fit into the expected behaviour, trying to please too much, I was trapped by a pretense of love and hypocrisy. We are human creatures, not perfect. People do make mistakes in their decisions, do fall back into old patterns of behaviour. We do have occasional natural aversions to others, which we should trust. We cannot pretend total love if it is not there. Insincerity is felt by others.

∞

THE NECESSITY OF CREATIVITY

I have found the repression of spirit in organized religion to be essentially a repression of my creativity, a squelching of my essence, resulting in my inability to see my own truth, my inability to speak my mind clearly. Using voice is a form of creation, but I was taught to feel shame if I spoke my mind clearly. I still have people try to shame me for it. Children were to be seen and not heard. Women, still, to the minds of many, should know their places, not speak out, not offend. Writing this, speaking my own truth, is one of the hardest things I have ever done in my life. It damns much of the principles in which I was raised. Writing this has been an agonized release for me, but so life-giving! What we are taught as children, what we are programmed to be, is so very important to our development. Creativity involves risk-taking. But conformity and adherence to duty and responsibility repress and squelch the creative spirit. If we were wrongly shamed as creative beings when we were young, then the very act of attempting to make art as adults creates shame in us. I found that I couldn't move forward with freedom in a religious setting. The ideas I formed from religious institutions have imprisoned me, and still do! My **Inside Suicide**!

Churches and religious institutions do not value creativity, or true individuality in thought and action. When they do make attempts in these directions, their efforts feel awkward and inhibited. Adherence to the code of the group always comes first. Individuality is allowed and encouraged within that range. Shame is triggered in us even as adults, when our internal censors stem from the ingrained patterns taught the child. Our internal speaker is still our creative child. When we are creating, or expressing ourselves in any form, if we have to continually consider whether we are doing right or wrong according to someone else's standards, how can we create? I have found letting my creativity come forth to be so difficult because my internal censor was so well trained by my family and community when I was a child. I learned very well to censor myself and my reactions when I was tiny. I have always judged myself according to others' views. It was wrong to offend. It is just now at this point in my life that I can recognize the damage that has been done to me. Children need to be raised with the freedom to make their own decisions, with wise and loving parents in the background as a safety net. We need to learn to live in safety in life, and, at the same time, without hesitation. A very difficult task for parents to help their children learn! Mary Martin says, in *Conduct in Question*, "It's more a matter of being allowed to be yourself, not just rising to the top."

Carolyn Heilbrun refers to Virginia Woolf's search for freedom:

> In Woolf's decision to express her society's deprivation of women, she had two major obstacles to fear. The first was the ridicule, misery, and anxiety the patriarchy holds in store for those who express their anger about the enforced destiny of women. That not even Leonard could understand this condemns not Leonard, but the profound influence of the system that has served men so well. Even today after two decades of feminism, young women shy away from an emphatic statement of anger at the patriarchy. Perhaps only women who have played the patriarchal game and won a self despite it can find the courage to consider facing the pain that the outright expression of feminism entails. *Heilbrun, (p.125)*

Throughout the centuries of our immediate history of patriarchal domination, women have had limited permissions to create. Men have been, and still are able to fulfill their own creative needs much more easily than women, for men can express themselves in whatever manner they wish. Seldom have women had the permission of our societies to create outside our homes, in economic settings in our communities: in business, in production, in the arts, in forging connections with others in society. Creativity is using one's energy to express oneself imaginatively, inventively in connecting with the world, making one's mark on it.

∞

FRIENDSHIP

Women need the companionship of other women in order to defeat the feeling of isolation in their struggles. We need to tell our stories, to be encouraged in our effort for understanding, for advancement. True friendship is having a friend in whom one can confide one's innermost thoughts about values in life, about how to live life well for oneself, without feeling judged. It is true respect for the other's views, even if they are not the views one would accept for oneself. True friendship is listening and empathizing. Belief in the other. True friendship requires the ability to let oneself become vulnerable in expressing one's deepest feelings about life. It is the awareness that these qualities are reciprocated in each other. This fosters self-worth on both sides. In friendship, differences do occur, as long as there is respect for the other's points of view.

Respect for others implies a connectedness to the rest of the world. There is a spirit which runs through all peoples and all things, which holds us in a oneness. The consciousness we have of this spirit derives from the so-called feminine side, from the right brain, from our love of life, of beauty in all we experience. This spirit is the force of life and love. As Sue Monk Kidd defines it:, "Goddess is that which unites, connects, and affirms the interrelatedness of all life, all people. Being related is at the core of Divine Feminine Being. She is the dance of relation, the mystery of the Divine communing with Herself in all things." (Kidd, p. 155)

∞

SELF-WORTH COMES FROM PERSONAL POWER

In order to live life fully, we need a sense of self-worth. When we give away our personal power to an institution like the church, then we often try to regain our power by controlling others, by judging negatively, as I did for a good portion of my life. As a result I am now able to see the faults for myself in how religious institutions have been, and are still wrong for me. By expressing my anger, I am finding that I am better able to let go of judging my friends and others who still see a need to find themselves in institutionalized religion. Anderson and Hopkins explain "....when we are in the process of moving away from someone or something that once nourished and sustained us, we often become critical or angry in order to garner enough energy to make the necessary separation." (Anderson and Hopkins, p. 61). Each person who goes through the process of self-discovery must find their own way.

Anderson and Hopkins really understand this: "....each woman [who undertook an internal search] had to come to terms with her own experience in all its particularities. If she judged herself too harshly because her behaviour and feeling did not correspond with what others - even those closest to her - seemed to be doing and feeling, she could not cross this threshold and accept the reality of her own life. Each woman had to be emotionally present in her own life and somehow find a way to trust *it*." Anderson and Hopkins, (p. 55)

What has been and is right for me, is not necessarily right for others. I respect this. Since I once believed the Church and its implicit and unavoidable dicta of sin and consequent guilt, to be the One True religious institution, guilt has been a necessary repercussion for me. I have found that I may still get a feeling of guilt, especially if I have felt belittled about my ability to control or influence a situation. But I have found that I can regain my power by letting others be as they wish, and as they need to be. Each person is in his or her own time and space. This is still difficult for me, for I was taught by my culture to judge. Now, I try hard not to judge others, to let go of my need to control situations. To change the ingrained patterns I was taught as a child is uphill work. **Climbing out from my Inside Suicide!** "Learning to trust the unfolding of one's own life is awkward, painful work that often leaves one feeling exposed and vulnerable. And it does not happen overnight." (Anderson and Hopkins, p. 55).

I have found that I can maintain my self-worth if I foster the following qualities within myself: intuition, common sense, and a realization of my own capabilities. Intuition: If a connection or situation *feels* wrong, I no longer go there from a sense of duty, loyalty, or a need to succeed. If a connection *feels* right, I try to risk it. I have learned not to hesitate by feeling I must protect myself. Common sense: Is this situation right for me in my circumstances? Will it harm me more than it will benefit me? Would I feel comfortable here? And finally, I have found that I need to realize my capabilities: Am I taking on too much, considering what I am physically, emotionally and intellectually capable of handling? Is this situation beyond me? Or will it stretch me as a person to become what I think I am capable of achieving? Understanding myself takes extreme honesty with others and with myself. Total honesty is extremely difficult! But it is the path to self-respect.

Going into myself to discover my truths, different from those imposed by family and friends, is very difficult work. To be myself compelled me to discover my own way. Anderson and Hopkins describe the process thusly: "We feel frightened, inept, confused. The familiar roles that have let us feel strong and sure of ourselves are gone, and along with them goes the predictability of our lives. To add to our insecurity, anxious friends and family are likely to ask: 'Why can't you be satisfied with things as they are?' and 'Aren't you afraid you'll regret this?'" (Anderson and Hopkins, p. 56)

To discover one's essence requires virtually cutting oneself off from family and society, from all of the familiar things and people: heart-rending, agonizing, terrifying work. Many women actually leave home physically in order to go into their own sacred depths. This work requires trust in oneself, and trust in a confidant. Some people are able to go through the process more quickly than I did. I have found it slow, uneven work, which I could only accomplish with the help of a therapist, who encouraged me to search for, and accept my own truths. I slowly discovered who I am, and what has molded me to become my current 'me'. I still find it difficult to trust my 'me', to enjoy myself as I am, to let myself express my ideas with confidence. To accept my limitations, and live with them. To trust in my own truths. To act on them. I find that if I am going through a stressful period of my life, it is much harder for me to do the work I have chosen for myself, and that I may halt, or even regress in my thinking patterns for a few weeks or months. If I am in a more stress-free period, I can be much more productive. "'Finally you see that there is nothing you can trust - nobody, no authority - except the process itself,' the spiritual teacher A. H. Almaas observes." (Anderson and Hopkins, p. 57.)

The spiritual force of the world, the Divine, the Goddess, is pure creativity. She is the energy of sex, of birth, of rebirth, of creativity, of transformation, of connection, of receptivity. We are not beings separate from the earth, but at one with it. We did not come into the earth; we came out of it. True spirit is not an outside force imposed upon us as a definite belief system. Belief systems caused **an Inside Suicide** for me. To experience the Divine is simply to be open to one's own spirit, and to disseminate it. This is true holiness. The Divine Force pervades all human beings, all living things, connecting us with each other. The Spirit comes from within us, from our connection to the natural world, from our abilities to create meaningful relationships with others. It comes from our joy in day-to-day living of our own lives, not in judging ourselves, or comparing ourselves to others. True Spirit comes from a deep self-respect, a respect for our own abilities to create and sustain life. It is a perception of the meaning of each life, and of one's responsibility to live as well as possible. True Spirit lives within each of us.

∞

The Journey

One day you finally knew
what you had to do, and began,
though the voices around you
kept shouting
their bad advice--
though the whole house
began to tremble
and you felt the old tug
at your ankles.
"Mend my life!"
each voice cried.
But you didn't stop.
You knew what you had to do,
though the wind pried
with its stiff fingers
at the very foundations,
though their melancholy
was terrible.
It was already late
enough, and a wild night,
and the road full of fallen
branches and stones.
But little by little,
as you left their voices behind,
the stars began to burn
through the sheets of clouds,
and there was a new voice
which you slowly
recognized as your own,
that kept you company
as you strode deeper and deeper
into the world,
determined to do

THE INSIDE SUICIDE: SHATTERING ILLUSIONS

the only thing you could do--
determined to save
the only life you could save.

Mary Oliver (Dream Work)

(Mary Oliver is an American poet who has won the National Book Award and the Pulitzer Prize).

∞

Bibliography

Anderson, Sherry Ruth and Patricia Hopkins. *The Feminine Face of God.* New York: Bantam Books, 1992.

Bolen, Jean Shinoda. *Crossing to Avalon.* San Francisco: HarperCollins, 1994.

Bradley, Marion Zimmer. *The Mists of Avalon.* New York: Ballantyne Books, 1982.

Eisler, Rianne. *The Chalice and the Blade.* New York: HarperCollins, 1987.

Estes, Clarissa Pinkola. *Warming the Stone Child.* (Cassette Tape)

Estes, Clarissa Pinkola. *Women Who Run With the Wolves.* Toronto Random House, 1992.

Harris, Joanne. *Chocolat.* Toronto: Doubleday, 2002.

Harris, Joanne. *Five Quarters of the Orange.* New York: William Morrow Publishing,. 2001.

Heilbrun, Carolyn G. *Writing a Woman's Life.* Toronto: Ballantyne, 2002.

Kidd, Sue Monk. *The Dance of the Dissident Daughter.* HarperSanFrancisco, 1996.

Kingsolver, Barbara. *The Poisonwood Bible.* Toronto: Harper Perennial, 1999.

Lamb, Wally. *I Know This Much Is True.* New York: HarperCollins, 1998.

Lerner, Harriet. G., Ph.D. *The Dance of Deception.* Toronto, Harper, 1993.

MacDonald, Ann Marie. *Fall on Your Knees.* New York: Simon & Schuster Inc.,1998.

Myss, Caroline. *Anatomy of the Spirit.* New York: Three Rivers Press, 1996.

Oates, Joyce Carol. *We Were the Mulvaneys.* New York: Plume Publishing, 1996.

Oliver, Mary. "The Journey," *New and Selected Poems.* p. 114. Boston: Beacon Press, 1992.

Pennington, Sheila. *The Dragon Within.* Toronto: Cybercom Publishing, 2002.

Pennington, Sheila. *Healing Yourself: Understanding How Your Mind Can Heal Your Body.* Toronto: McGraw-Hill Ryerson, 1988.

Pirsig, Robert M. *Zen and the Art of Motorcycle Maintenance: An Inquiry into Values.* Bantam Books, 1984.

Shields, Carol. *Unless.* Toronto: Random House of Canada Limited, 2002.

Sjoo, Monica and Barbara Mor. *The Great Cosmic Mother.* HarperSanFrancisco, 1991.

Stone, Merlin. *When God Was a Woman.* Toronto: Harcourt, Inc., 1976.

Winter, Miriam Therese. *WomanWisdom.* New York: The Crossroad Publishing Company, 1991.

Winter, Miriam Therese. *WomanWitness.* New York: The Crossroad Publishing Company, 1992.

Winter, Miriam Therese. *WomanWord.* New York: The Crossroad Publishing Company, 1990.

INDEX

Afghanistan, 34, 70, 83
Anatolia, 18
Anglican, 53
Anne Sexton, 28
Apuleius, 21
Arabia, 18
Aristotle Onassis, 12
Astarte, 20
Athenians, 21
Au Set, 21
Australia, 18
Babylonians, 20
Baptist, 57
Barbara Kingsolver, 70
Bellona, 21
Bellona of the Battles, 21
Bertrand Russell, 69
bible, 35
Carolyn G. Heilbrun, 8
Carolyn Myss, 90
Catholic church, 48
Cecropian Artemis, 21
Charles Darwin, 55
Christian, 3, 7, 9, 10, 11, 13, 14, 25, 27, 31, 33, 34, 40, 43, 50, 53, 54, 55, 57, 61, 62, 63, 79, 81, 89
Cyprus, 21
Demeter, 19
Dictynna, 21
École Polytechnique, 61
Egyptian Goddess, 21
Egyptians, 21
Eisler, 19, 20, 22, 103
Eleusinians, 21
Eskimos, 18
Eve, 35, 61
Genesis, 61
George Eliot, 68
George Sands, 68
God as a Woman, 18

H. Almaas, 100
Heilbrun, 23, 27, 28, 32, 33, 56, 58, 85, 96, 103
Helen of Troy, 83
Hesiod, 19
Ishtar, 20
Jacqueline Kennedy, 12
Japanese, 18
John F. Kennedy, 12
Joyce Carol Oates, 43
Judaism, 18, 20, 50
Judeo-Christian, 73
June Callwood, 37
June Singer, 31
Jungian, 15, 31, 63
Juno, 21
Khasis of India, 18
Kore, 19
Kurgians, 20
Louise Hay, 90
Macbeth, 5
Maria Callas, 12
Merlin Stone, 18, 20
Middle Ages, 34, 61
Muslim, 34, 62, 73
Neolithic, 20, 21
Northrop Frye, 28
Origin of Species, 55
Paleolithic, 20
Paphian Aphrodite, 21
Patriarchy, 15
Patricia Hopkins, 3, 92, 103
Pessinuntica, 21
Phoenicia, 20
Phrygians, 21
Queen Isis, 21
Renaissance, 73, 83
Rhamnubia, 21
rheumatoid arthritis, 56, 94
Riane Eisler, 18, 19, 21

THE INSIDE SUICIDE: SHATTERING ILLUSIONS

Robert Graves, 21
Robert J. Pirsig, 26
Roman Catholic, 29, 48, 53
Romance of the Rose, 73
Sacred Feminine, 23
Salem, 34
Semites, 20
Sheila Pennington, 90
Sherry Ruth Anderson, 3, 92
Sicilians, 21
Stygian Proserpine, 21
Sue Monk Kidd, 11, 13, 15, 22, 23, 31, 97

Sylvia Perera, 15
Tao Te Ching, 19
The Divine Force, 100
The One and Only Truth!, 47
Twylah Nitsch, 92
United Church, 7, 54, 72
United Church of Canada, 7
Veneration, 21
Willa Cather, 68
witchcraft, 34
Wuthering Heights, 5

THE INSIDE SUICIDE: SHATTERING ILLUSIONS
Rosemary L. Golding

(Photo by Ben Harrison)

Rosemary Golding lives with her husband in Orillia Ontario. She has an Honours B.A. in Philosophy and English, and an M.A. in English. Before she retired, she taught high school English in several boards of education in Ontario for more than thirty years.

In this autobiographical retrospective, Rosemary examines the influences in her life that determine who she is today.

This book will be of great value and support to any person struggling with an awareness of unfulfilled challenges and opportunities, anyone who has a desire to understand who they are, and how they developed in this way. This book will suggest various options for making positive changes in life.

∞

THE INSIDE SUICIDE: SHATTERING ILLUSIONS

CPSIA information can be obtained at www.ICGtesting.com
Printed in the USA
LVOW071945141212

311729LV00002B/2/P

9 780981 359380